THE NEW BLENDER BOOK

Barbara Karoff

BRISTOL PUBLISHING ENTERPRISES
San Leandro, California

A Nitty Gritty® Cookbook

Printed in the United States of America.

ISBN 1-55867-088-2

Cover design: Frank Paredes
Front cover photography: John Benson
Food stylist: Suzanne Carreiro
Illustrator: James Balkovek

CONTENTS

Dedicated to my father, a come-lately cook who is doing quite well, thank you.

I extend my gratitude to my family and friends who once again encouraged me with their support and their favorite recipes. Special thanks to my sons, David, Paul and John, to my daughter-in-law, Linda, to my sister, Joyce Dutton and to my good friends, Nan Dowd and Nancy Gerst.
A very special thank you to my "technical advisor," Bob Simmons.

ABOUT BLENDERS

Although blenders have been a dependable kitchen standby for over 50 years, the 1990s are bringing us an unprecedented "blender boom." New manufacturers, new features and new and improved models are all helping consumers to rediscover the usefulness and the versatility of the blender. We've come a long way since band leader Fred Waring promoted the original blender to success.

Fred Waring did not invent the blender, although he is often given credit, but he did recognize the potential of a good idea and decided to back the prototype product brought to him by inventer Fred Osius. Through Waring's efforts, the machine was introduced as the "Miracle Mixer" at the National Restaurant Show in Chicago in 1937. It was an instant hit.

Despite the fact that their overall success has been phenomenal, for a number of recent years blenders have been overshadowed by food processors, the glamorous new kids in the kitchen. This state of affairs is finally changing as experienced cooks recognize an important fact. One of these appliances does not replace the other. They perform different tasks in our modern kitchens and, if properly used, they compliment one another beautifully.

There is, of course, some overlap, a few jobs that both the blender and the food processor do equally well, but for the most part, they each have their own territories. It is a major mistake to expect a blender to do all that a food processor does. The blender is a different piece of equipment and it was designed to function differently.

THE BLENDER IS YOUR BEST BET FOR MANY TASKS

Blenders puree and liquefy foods to a smoothness no food processor can match. For a velvety textured soup or sauce, the blender has no peer.

Most blenders whip cream without a special attachment, make cracker crumbs for crusts and bread crumbs for toppings and fillers, grate hard cheese, grate fresh coconut, mix frozen juices, chop nuts, raisins and softened dried fruits and grind coffee beans. Many of the new machines crush ice without the addition of water. All models are perfect for removing lumps from gravies and sauces.

With many manufacturers currently beefing up the market with a wide range of both new and improved blenders, it is not the purpose of this book to detail the specific functions of each model. Every blender comes with literature that explicitly details its particular capabilities. It is extremely important to read this information carefully. To get the maximum performance from any appliance, you must know what the manufacturer has built it to do.

I will, instead, offer you recipes and tips to help you get the most use and the most delicious results from your blender. I have little patience with books and recipes that serve only as excuses to use a blender or that call for doing something in a blender that, while the machine will do the job, could be more efficiently accomplished another way.

The recipes in this collection call for the use of a blender because it makes the best sense. In each case, it is, I believe, the most efficient way to accomplish the required result.

BLENDERS, GOOD HEALTH AND HOME ENTERTAINING

One of the major reasons for the revival of interest in blenders is the health connection. This clarion call of the 1990s puts the blender in line for a permanent position on your kitchen counter.

Healthy drinks, often called smoothies, top the list. Fruit- and dairy product-based, these simple-to-whip-up meals can be made to incorporate extra doses of vitamins, fiber and protein and to send you off for a day properly and quickly prepared.

Vegetables and fruit purees, quickly made in a blender, are invaluable for thickening and flavoring sauces, stews and soups without adding flour. Or, try adding a thick vegetable puree to a broth to create a flavorful and healthy sauce.

Healthy, preservative-free dips and spreads are easy with a blender to puree specially purchased or left over ingredients.

Baby foods made in the blender, and made with the foods that you choose, are baby-friendly, silky smooth and minus offending lumps. When you make your own baby foods, you also have the option of adding extra vitamins, eggs, formula or fruit and vegetable juices to whatever you prepare. Homemade baby foods are the perfect way to introduce family table food to the young eater at an early age.

Home entertaining also gets a boost when a blender is in the kitchen. Smooth flavorful dips are a blender specialty. Velvety soups are perfect every time. Salad dressings, mayonnaise and other sauces are ready, fresh and flavorful in minutes. Delicious sorbets, ice creams and specialty drinks will all help put the spotlight on your culinary star.

HOW TO USE YOUR BLENDER

Many blender models have only two speeds, high and low. Many others have combinations of speeds covering a wide range of functions. Because of these differences, I have not specified number or function buttons in this book. In general, however, low speed is equal to numbers one through seven and high speed is equal to numbers eight through fourteen. Also, in general, the speed you choose should be determined by the density of what is to be blended. And, it goes without saying, that if you begin at low or at a number between one and seven and not much happens, you should up the speed.

Again, each blender manufacturer will tell you exactly how to use its product and you should read all manufacturer's instructions carefully. In general, however, the speed suggestions I have mentioned, and the following do's and don't's, are useful to keep in mind.

- Do put liquid ingredients in the blender before adding dry ingredients unless a recipe specifically directs otherwise.
- Do cut firm food into pieces no larger than 1 inch before blending.
- Do cut all cheese into pieces no larger than ½ inch before blending.
- Do, always, start the motor with the cover securely on the container.
- Do turn the motor off immediately if it stalls or seems overworked.
- Do stop frequently while blending to scrape down the sides of the blender container.
- Do make sure the motor is completely stopped before using a spatula or any utensil in the blender.
- Do remove the center section of the two-piece lid when blending hot ingredients.
- Do start blending on low speed except when blending very heavy foods. Then start on high.
- Do make sure the motor is completely stopped before removing the container from the base.

- Do not overload the blender. Half full is enough (unless your manufacturer's instructions state otherwise). Do large amounts in several batches.

- Do not store foods in the blender container. Always wash and dry the container thoroughly after each use.

- Do not ever leave a blender while it is operating.

- Do not expect a blender to do jobs it is not designed to do. It will not: mash potatoes, whip egg whites, grind raw meats, knead or mix stiff doughs or extract juices from fruits and vegetables.

- Do not overblend. The blender is designed to be a fast working machine and most tasks are accomplished quickly.

INGREDIENTS

A note about ingredients called for in the recipes that follow: Although they represent personal choices, (and are not unbreakable rules) they are ones that have proven right for me over the years. Unless otherwise noted, I always use: unsalted (sweet) butter, Italian flat leaf parsley, freshly squeezed orange, lemon and lime juices, fresh basil, freshly grated pepper and nutmeg, (and other freshly ground spices whenever possible) kosher salt and canola or olive oil unless another is specifically called for to add flavor.

A number of recipes in this book call for roasted peppers and for roasted garlic. The following procedures reveal the simple how-to secrets.

To roast bell peppers and chili peppers on a gas stove: Place peppers directly on the gas flame. With kitchen tongs, turn them until they are completely black. Transfer peppers to a paper bag, close it up and let peppers steam for about 10 minutes. Remove from the bag and the skins, which are now black, will slip off.

To roast peppers on an electric stove: Place peppers on a baking sheet directly under the broiler. Broil, turning frequently, until peppers are completely black. Transfer peppers to a paper bag, close it up and let peppers steam for about 10 minutes. Remove from the bag and the skins, which are now black, will slip off.

To roast garlic: Preheat oven to 350°. Trim the tops off one or several heads of garlic. Place garlic in a shallow baking dish and drizzle with olive oil. Sprinkle with salt and pepper. Roast for 30 minutes. Reduce the temperature to 250° and continue to roast for 1 hour. Cool and squeeze soft garlic from skins.

Another method: Wrap whole, unpeeled heads of garlic tightly in foil. Place on a baking sheet and bake at 425° for 1 hour. Cool and squeeze soft garlic from skins.

How to make bread crumbs: To make either fresh or dried bread crumbs, cut or tear bread into small pieces. Add them to the blender while the motor is running, a slice at a time. If doing a large amount, empty the crumbs from the blender after 2 or 3 slices and continue. One slice of bread makes about ½ cup of crumbs.

Tips for making baby foods in the blender:

- Meats and vegetables can be blended raw, and then cooked in a saucepan, or you may simply blend cooked meats and vegetables.
- Process fruits and vegetables, either fresh, frozen or canned, with a small amount of fruit juice, milk, water or yogurt.
- Process meat, cooked or raw, with a small amount of vegetable juice, broth, water or yogurt.
- General rule (varies with moisture content of foods used): For ¾ cup fruit, use 2 tsp. liquid. For ½ cup meat or vegetables, use 4-6 tbs. liquid.
- Try combining meat and vegetables for a " one-dish meal."

Now — with these many words behind us — if you haven't used your blender in years, get it out, set it on the counter and put it to use. If you do not own a blender, now is the time to check over the newly available, expanded selection. A blender in your kitchen is a wonderful investment in saving time. Much more important, it is an investment in your good health and, with the recipes that follow, in your good eating as well. Bon Appetit.

DRESSINGS, DIPS AND SPREADS

CLASSIC VINAIGRETTE

A classic vinaigrette is little more than oil and vinegar, generally three parts oil to one part vinegar, minced garlic and/or shallot, Dijon or dry mustard and salt and pepper to taste. Some people like to add a spoonful or so of cream to cut the acidity.

Simply combine all the ingredients in the blender, which will create an emulsion that will hold up for several days. If it breaks down, reblend.

VARIATIONS

Use different oils and vinegars or substitute lemon juice for all or part of the vinegar. Very intense oils (some olive oils and some nut oils) are best used in combination with a mild oil such as canola.

- **Herb Vinaigrette:** Add basil, tarragon, dill, mint or any herb that compliments your salad.
- **Red Onion Vinaigrette:** Add minced red onion instead of shallots.
- **Cilantro-Cumin Vinaigrette:** Add these congenial seasonings to the basic recipe and substitute lemon juice for the vinegar.

OLD STANDBY FRENCH DRESSING
Yield: about 1 cup

Try this old favorite with grapefruit and avocado salad.

½ medium onion, cut into pieces
1 tsp. salt
1 tbs. sugar
1 tsp. paprika
2 tsp. Dijon mustard

½ tsp. Worcestershire sauce
½ cup catsup
½ cup canola oil
1 clove garlic, pressed, optional

Puree onion in the blender. Add remaining ingredients except oil and garlic; blend thoroughly. With motor running, add oil in a slow stream. If using garlic, stir in.

CHINESE CHICKEN SALAD DRESSING
Yield: about 1½ cups

Serve this tangy dressing on a salad of poached and shredded chicken. Add the oil carefully and only enough to create a proper emulsion.

4 tbs. lemon juice
⅔ cup soy sauce
2 tsp. dry mustard

2 tsp. ground ginger
2 dashes Tabasco Sauce
⅔ cup (approximately) peanut oil

Put lemon juice, soy sauce, mustard, ginger and Tabasco in the blender. With motor running, add oil in a stream to form a thick but pourable dressing.

LINDA'S SPECIAL SALAD DRESSING

Yield: about 1 cup

This special dressing is made to order for a salad of romaine lettuce, fresh strawberries and red onion. Yes, it's unusual, but the combination is terrific.

½ cup mayonnaise
2 tbs. cider vinegar
⅓ cup sugar

¼ cup milk
2 tbs. poppy seeds

Place all ingredients in the blender and blend until smooth.

SALAD INGREDIENTS

1-2 heads romaine lettuce, rinsed, dried
1 quart strawberries, rinsed, stemmed,
 sliced

1 medium red onion, very thinly sliced

Tear lettuce into bite-sized pieces. Put into salad bowl with strawberries and onion. Pour dressing over and toss well.

GARBANZO SALAD DRESSING

Yield: about 1 cup

Because I'm so fond of garbanzo beans, this dressing is an all-time favorite of mine. It's great on any vegetable salad but superb with fresh, ripe summer tomatoes.

1 can (15 oz.) garbanzo beans
1/4 cup lemon juice
2 cloves garlic, minced

1/2 cup canola oil
salt

In the blender, place beans, with their liquid, lemon juice and garlic; puree until smooth. With motor running, slowly add oil. Season to taste with salt.

TOFU-BLUE CHEESE DRESSING

Yield: about 1 cup

This healthy, creamy dressing is especially good on a romaine salad.

1/4 cup plain yogurt
1/2 cup tofu
2 tsp. white wine or rice wine vinegar
4 tbs. blue cheese

1 clove garlic, cut into pieces
salt and pepper
milk to thin

Combine yogurt, tofu, vinegar, blue cheese and garlic in the blender and process until smooth. Transfer to a bowl. Add salt and pepper to taste. Thin with milk if necessary.

THAI SATE MARINADE

Yield: about 2 cups

This spicy Thai marinade turns small bites of pork or chicken into irresistible appetizers or party nibbles. Or, serve several skewers on a plate for a tasty entrée. Watch the red pepper flakes if you're not used to them. They pack a fiery punch.

1 cup salted peanuts
2 tbs. ground coriander
2 cloves garlic
½ -1 tsp. red pepper flakes
1 cup chopped onion
¼ cup lemon juice

2 tbs. brown sugar
¼ cup soy sauce
½ cup chicken stock
½ cup butter or margarine
2 lb. lean pork or chicken

Place all ingredients except butter and meat in the blender and blend to a smooth puree. Do in several batches, if necessary. Transfer puree to a saucepan, add butter and heat until butter is melted. Cool.

Pour cooled sauce over 2 lb. lean pork or chicken cut into 1-inch cubes. Marinate at least 3 hours. Thread meat on bamboo skewers (which have been soaked in water for 1 hour) and broil or grill, turning frequently to brown and cook evenly. Heat leftover sauce to serve with meat, if desired.

VINAIGRETTE FOR COOKING BLACK BEANS

Two cups of dried black beans cooked in water with this puree are wonderfully flavorful and ready for salad — a South-of-the-Border treat.

1 large onion, cut into pieces
3-4 cloves garlic, cut into pieces
3 jalapeños, stemmed, seeded, cut into pieces
15 sprigs cilantro
1 cup water
2 cups dry black beans

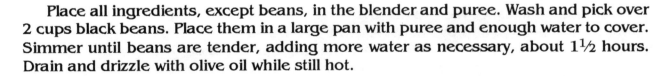

Place all ingredients, except beans, in the blender and puree. Wash and pick over 2 cups black beans. Place them in a large pan with puree and enough water to cover. Simmer until beans are tender, adding more water as necessary, about 1½ hours. Drain and drizzle with olive oil while still hot.

PATÉ MOLD

Although this recipe calls for canned condensed beef broth, substitute an equal amount of good hearty homemade stock if you have it. This is a great make-ahead appetizer for a large party.

1 envelope unflavored gelatin
1 can (10¾ oz.) condensed beef broth
½ tsp. Tabasco Sauce
½ lb. chicken livers
1 tbs. butter

1 cup sour cream
2 tbs. coarsely chopped onion
2 tbs. chopped parsley
½ cup chopped black olives

In a saucepan, sprinkle gelatin over half the broth. Cook over low heat for 5 minutes, stirring constantly. Remove from heat and stir in remaining broth and Tabasco Sauce. Sauté chicken livers in butter until just cooked through. Cut them in pieces, if very large, and place in the blender with sour cream and onions. Puree until smooth. Add parsley and run motor just long enough to incorporate.

Transfer mixture to a bowl and stir in broth and olives. Mix well. Pour into a well-oiled 1-quart mold and chill until firm. Unmold at serving time and surround with crackers or toast rounds.

BLUE CHEESE APPETIZER SOUFFLÉ

Yield: 1½ cups

This appetizer soufflé is a beautiful presentation for a party. Serve it with raw vegetables or toasted baguette rounds.

1 envelope unflavored gelatin
2 tbs. cold water
4 tbs. butter, very soft, cut into pieces
4 tbs. cream cheese, very soft, cut into pieces
4 tbs. blue cheese, very soft, cut into pieces
1 egg, separated
1 tsp. Dijon mustard
½ cup heavy cream

In a saucepan, soften gelatin in cold water. Heat over low heat, stirring to dissolve. In the blender, in 2 batches, combine gelatin, butter, cream cheese, blue cheese, egg yolk and mustard. Transfer to a bowl. Beat cream to soft peaks and fold in. Fasten a foil collar around outside top of a 1-cup soufflé dish or straight-sided bowl. Spoon cheese mixture into dish so it comes to top of collar. Chill at least 3 hours. Remove collar carefully to serve.

PIMIENTO MOUSSE

Servings: 4 - 6

Plump, fleshy pimientos are more and more frequently sold fresh in our markets. Their rich flavor makes this appetizer or side dish mousse a special treat.

4 pimientos, roasted (see page 7), peeled, seeded, cut into pieces
1 clove garlic, sliced
¼ tsp. thyme
1 tbs. butter
1 tbs. white wine vinegar
⅔ cup heavy cream
salt

Sauté pimientos, garlic and thyme in butter over low heat for 20 minutes. Stir frequently. Add vinegar. Increase heat and cook until liquid has evaporated. Transfer mixture to the blender and puree. Transfer to a bowl. Beat cream until it holds soft peaks and fold it into pimiento puree. Add salt to taste. Serve with crusty baguette rounds.

LAYERED CHEESE TORTA

Yield: about 4 cups

This delicious torta makes a dramatic party presentation. Make it in a deep, straight-sided bowl or in a clean, new flower pot.

2 pkg. (8 oz. each) cream cheese, very soft, cut into pieces
2 cubes butter, very soft, cut into pieces
3¼ cups lightly packed fresh basil leaves
1½ cups freshly grated Parmesan cheese
½ cup olive oil
2-3 cloves garlic, cut into pieces
salt and pepper

In several batches, combine cream cheese and butter in the blender until it is very smooth. Transfer to a bowl and set aside.

Wash and dry blender container and add basil, Parmesan cheese, olive oil and garlic. Process to a smooth puree. Transfer to a second bowl and add salt and pepper to taste.

Dampen a square of cheesecloth, ring it out and, with it, carefully line bowl or flower pot. Try to have as few wrinkles and overlaps as possible. Place something edible and attractive in bottom of dish on top of the cheesecloth (a nasturtium flower, a pinwheel of green or red pepper slivers or paper thin slices of lemon). With a rubber spatula, spread a layer of cheese mixture in bottom. Cover with a thinner layer of pesto mixture. Repeat alternating layers, ending with cheese and taking care to spread layers to sides of mold. Fold ends of cheesecloth over and press down gently with hands.

Refrigerate 1 to 2 hours and then invert onto a serving dish and carefully remove cheesecloth. (If allowed to stand longer, the cheesecloth will cause the filling color to run.) Cover with plastic wrap and refrigerate until ready to serve.

YOGURT ARTICHOKE DIP

Yield: about 2 cups

This savory dip is great with tortilla chips or stuffed into pita bread with thick-sliced tomatoes.

1 cup plain yogurt
½ cup cottage cheese
½ cup marinated artichoke hearts, cut into pieces
2 green onions, cut into pieces
2 tsp. minced cilantro or parsley
salt and pepper

Combine all ingredients except salt and pepper in the blender. Add salt and pepper to taste. Serve at room temperature.

PAUL'S BABA GANNOUJ

Yield: about 1½ cups

For the uninitiated, this favorite Turkish dip is pronounced Baba Ga Noosh. For the initiated, just pass it around again, please.

1 eggplant, about ¾ lb.
2 cloves garlic, cut into pieces
2 tbs. lemon juice
¼ cup tahini (sesame paste)
1 tbs. olive oil
3 tbs. minced parsley

Bake eggplant in a 400° oven (on a baking sheet) or roast over a charcoal grill until it wilts and is soft throughout, about 25 minutes. When cool, scrape flesh away from skin and discard skin. There should be about 1 cup flesh. Place eggplant and garlic in the blender and blend to a smooth puree. Add remaining ingredients and blend again to a smooth puree. Serve with toasted pita bread triangles.

ROASTED GARLIC AND RED PEPPER DIP FOR VEGETABLES

Yield: about 2 cups

Roasting the peppers and garlic gives this dip a wonderful robust flavor. (See roasting methods, page 7). Try it on a composed salad of shrimp, avocado and endive, as a dip for crudites or with steamed artichokes.

2 roasted red bell peppers, seeded, cut into pieces
1 head garlic, roasted, pressed out (discard skins)
5 oz. mild goat cheese or cream cheese
3 tbs. olive oil
5 tbs. minced fresh basil
1 tsp. fresh rosemary
salt and pepper

Place all ingredients in the blender and mix to a smooth puree. Correct seasoning, if necessary, and refrigerate to firm.

OLIVE AIOLI

Yield: about 1½ cups

This versatile spread-dip-condiment from the south of France is best made early in the day or the day before so the flavors have a chance to blend. Use it with crudites, steamed vegetables and potatoes, artichokes, cold fish or as a spread for toasted baguette slices. The olives are an extra touch and the flavorful Mediterranean varieties are a better match for this assertive sauce than our domestic ones.

1 tsp. lemon juice
2-3 cloves garlic, cut into pieces
1 egg
½ tsp. Dijon mustard
1 cup (approximately) combination olive and canola oil
salt
20 olives, pitted, minced

Combine lemon juice, garlic, egg and mustard in the blender and blend to combine thoroughly. With motor running, add oil in a slow stream until mixture is a thick mayonnaise. Add salt to taste. Transfer to a bowl and chill several hours. Just before serving, gently stir in minced olives.

CHILI PEPPER DIP

This versatile dip is made to order for chips and raw vegetables. It's also good on seafood, as a salad dressing, with artichokes or drizzled over sliced tomatoes.

3 pasilla chilies, roasted (see page 7)
1 jalapeño chili, stemmed, seeded, cut into pieces
2 oz. cream cheese, room temperature
½ cup sour cream
several sprigs cilantro
pinch of oregano
salt

Remove stems from pasilla chilies. Peel, seed and cut into pieces. Place all ingredients except salt in the blender. Blend until completely smooth. Transfer to a bowl and add salt to taste. Garnish with additional cilantro if used as a dip.

SPICY EGGPLANT DIP

Yield: about 2 cups

This recipe calls for crushed red pepper flakes, an ingredient which should be used with discretion.

1 large eggplant
1-2 cloves garlic, cut into pieces
2 tbs. soy sauce
2 tbs. dry vermouth
1 tbs. minced ginger root
1 tbs. sesame oil
1 tbs. minced cilantro
crushed red pepper flakes
salt

Cut off eggplant stem. Pierce deeply all over with a fork. Place on a baking sheet and bake at 350° until it is very soft, about 1 hour. Slice eggplant in half when cool enough to handle and scoop flesh from skin. Place flesh, garlic, soy sauce, vermouth, ginger, sesame oil and cilantro in the blender and blend to a smooth puree. Remove to a bowl and add crushed red pepper flakes and salt to taste. Serve with crackers.

CREAMY TAPENADE

Yield: about 1 cup

A tapenade is a thick paste made from olives, olive oil, lemon juice and seasonings. This is not a traditional tapenade because the olive mixture is combined with cream cheese. Put the finished product in a small ramekin and serve with crackers or toasted rounds of baguette.

2 cloves garlic, cut into pieces
1½ cups pitted Kalamata olives
3 tbs. capers, drained
½ tsp. oregano
½ tsp. rosemary
2 tbs. olive oil
2 oz. cream cheese, room temperature, cut into pieces
salt and pepper

In the blender, combine garlic, olives, capers, oregano, rosemary, oil and cream cheese. Blend and scrape sides until mixture is coarsely ground. Transfer to a ramekin or other serving dish. Add salt and pepper to taste. Serve at room temperature.

HUMMUS

This Middle Eastern dip dates to ancient times. The blender makes it easily and to perfection. Be sure to prepare it at least several hours before you plan to use it so the flavors have a chance to blend.

1 can (15 oz.) garbanzo beans, drained
⅓ cup lemon juice
½ cup tahini (sesame paste)
3 tbs. chopped green onion
2 cloves garlic, cut into pieces
salt and pepper
cilantro or parsley for garnish

Combine all ingredients, except salt, pepper and cilantro, in the blender. It may be necessary to add a small amount of water, but add only enough to blend mixture to a smooth, thick puree. Transfer to a bowl, add salt and pepper to taste and chill. Garnish with cilantro and serve with triangles of toasted pita bread or plain crackers.

COTTAGE CHEESE "CHEESE"

Yield: about 2 cups

This is a great make-ahead. Enjoy it with your favorite fruit as a light dessert — or for breakfast or a snack.

½-1 cup milk
2 cups cottage cheese

honey to taste
fruit of choice, fresh or frozen

Place ⅓ cup of milk in the blender and, with motor running, gradually add cottage cheese. Add more milk, if necessary, to form a fairly thick puree. Add honey to taste and puree until smooth. Spoon into containers and refrigerate. The longer it sits, the thicker it becomes. To serve, stir pieces of fruit or berries into cheese. If using frozen fruit, stir in while still frozen so that juices are released into cheese.

DEVILED MEAT SANDWICH SPREAD

Yield: about 1½ cups

A great way to use leftover meat for a tasty sandwich spread.

1 cup cooked meat (ham, beef, chicken)
1 slice onion

¼ cup mayonnaise

Put all ingredients in the blender and process until smooth. Depending on meat, add chopped pickle, curry powder, herbs and/or salt and pepper to taste.

FRUIT SANDWICH SPREAD

Out of jam at sandwich making time? Your blender can help you create a spread you may enjoy even more. Softened dried fruit, one kind or several, combined in the blender with a small amount of fruit juice, honey and/or nuts makes a delicious spread for sandwiches or toast.

NUT BUTTERS
Yield: ¾ cup

Make your own peanut butter. Try almond, hazelnut and cashew nut butters, too.

1½ cup salted nuts

Place nuts in the blender and process to a smooth consistency. Scrape frequently with a rubber spatula to keep nuts around blades and processing well.

SOUPS

Pureed vegetable and pureed bean soups are usually simple and delicious. Their variety is limited only by the vegetables or beans at hand. Some versions call for a final enrichment of *Creme Fraiche*, sweet cream, sour cream or yogurt. Others rely on olive oil, minced raw vegetables, spices, herbs or cheese to enhance their flavor. Some recipes, especially those made with beans, call for pureeing only half of the cooked soup and combining the pureed and unpureed halves, thus creating a more textured final dish. If you prefer a completely smooth puree, your blender will do the job.

CREAM OF VEGETABLE SOUP NORMANDY   Servings: 6

This recipe calls for sweating the vegetables, a process which cooks them to soft perfection without browning. It also calls for Creme Fraiche, easily made.

2 carrots, peeled, thinly sliced
10 leeks, white part only, thinly sliced
3 turnips, peeled, thinly sliced
4 tbs. butter

6 potatoes, peeled, thinly sliced
8 cups chicken stock
salt and pepper
1 cup *Creme Fraiche*, follows

Sweat carrots, leeks and turnips in butter for 20 minutes. (Melt butter in a soup pot. Add vegetables. Cover with a round of waxed paper. Cover pot and cook over very low heat.) Remove waxed paper, add potatoes and stock and bring to a boil. Reduce heat and simmer for 45 minutes. Puree in small batches in the blender. Add salt and pepper to taste and 1 cup *Creme Fraiche*. Mix well. Bring just to a boil and serve at once.

CREME FRAICHE   Yield: 1 cup

1 cup heavy cream   2½ tsp. buttermilk

Place cream and buttermilk in a jar. Cover and shake for 1 minute. Let stand at room temperature for at least 8 hours or until it is very thick. Shake again and refrigerate. Will keep, refrigerated, for 4 to 6 weeks.

CREAM OF VEGETABLE SOUP VARIATION

Servings: 6

*This soup uses the same methods as **Cream of Vegetable Soup Normandy** but different vegetables. It illustrates that whatever is on hand will probably produce a delicious soup, so don't be afraid to experiment.*

$^1/_2$ head red cabbage, shredded
3 leeks, with some green, thinly sliced
1 carrot, peeled, thinly sliced
4 tbs. butter
2 potatoes, peeled and thinly sliced
$^1/_2$-$^3/_4$ can (28 oz.) tomatoes, with juice
8 cups chicken stock
salt and pepper
1 cup *Creme Fraiche*, page 33

Sweat cabbage, leeks and carrot in butter for 20 minutes (see page 33). Remove waxed paper and add potatoes, tomatoes and stock. Bring to a boil, reduce heat and simmer for 45 minutes. Puree in small batches in the blender. Add salt and pepper to taste and 1 cup *Creme Fraiche*. Mix well. Bring just to a boil and serve at once.

ROOT VEGETABLE SOUP

Servings: 6

Proportions in this hearty winter recipe need not be followed exactly.

5 tbs. butter
2 onions, chopped
2 cloves garlic, cut into pieces
2 parsnips, diced
2 carrots, peeled, sliced
1 small celery root, peeled, diced, optional
3 potatoes, peeled, diced
2 turnips, diced
6 cups chicken stock
salt and pepper
half and half

Melt butter in a soup pot. Add onion and garlic and cook for 5 minutes. Add parsnips, carrots, celery root, potatoes, turnips and stock. Bring to a boil, reduce heat and simmer until vegetables are very tender, about 45 minutes. Puree in the blender in small batches. Add salt and pepper to taste and thin to desired consistency with half and half. Heat just to a boil and serve at once.

CREAM OF CAULIFLOWER AND LEEK SOUP   Servings: 4

Cauliflower and leeks are a wonderful flavor blend. This hearty soup, enriched with egg yolks and half and half, is delicious, hot or cold.

1 small cauliflower, cut into florets
4-6 leeks, white part only, minced
4 tbs. butter
4 cups chicken stock
2 egg yolks
1 cup half and half
salt and pepper

Place cauliflower in cold water to cover. Heat to a boil, reduce heat and cook for 1 minute. Drain and refresh in cold water. Sauté leeks in butter until soft. Add cauliflower and stock. Cook, uncovered, over medium heat for 30 minutes. Puree in the blender in small batches. Return soup to pot and heat just to a boil. Remove from heat. Whisk egg yolks into half and half. Whisk $1/3$ cup of the soup mixture into egg mixture. Whisk egg-soup mixture into hot soup; cook and stir for 2 minutes. Serve hot or cold.

PUREED ORANGE-CARROT SOUP

Servings: 6

How can something this good for you also taste this good? Well, it just does. Serve it icy cold and, if you want to be fancy, in a stemmed glass.

½ tsp. peeled, minced ginger root
6 carrots, peeled, thinly sliced
1 leek, white part only, thinly sliced
2 tbs. canola oil
3 cups chicken stock
1½ cups freshly squeezed orange juice
salt and pepper
mint leaves for garnish

Sauté ginger, carrots and leek in oil until carrots are soft. Add 2 cups stock and simmer 30 minutes. Puree in the blender in small batches. Add remaining stock, orange juice and salt and pepper to taste. Chill for at least 4 hours.

NOTE: It is best not to use a fat that will solidify when cold (such as butter) when making cold soups.

VICHYSSOUISE

Despite its French name, Vichyssouise is an all-American soup. The blender makes it to velvety perfection.

4 large onions, sliced
2 tbs. canola oil
3 baking potatoes, peeled, diced
3 cups chicken stock
2 cups half and half
1 cup milk
salt and pepper
chopped fresh chives for garnish

Sauté onions in oil until soft but not brown. Add potatoes and stock and simmer, covered, for 45 minutes or until potatoes are very soft. Puree in small batches in the blender. Chill. At serving time, stir in half and half, milk and salt and pepper to taste. Garnish with chopped chives.

MOROCCAN FAVA BEAN SOUP

Servings: 6

Fava beans are labor-intensive because each bean must be peeled. Their exceptionally rich flavor, however, makes the effort worth the time it takes.

1⅓ cups dried fava beans
3½ cups water
3 cloves garlic
⅓ cup olive oil
⅓ tbs. cumin, or to taste
⅓ tbs. sweet paprika
2 tbs. lemon juice
salt and pepper

Soak beans in water to cover overnight. Drain. Peel outer brown skin off each bean. Bring 3½ cups water to a boil. Add beans and garlic and simmer until beans are very tender, about 1½ hours. Add more water, if necessary. Puree in the blender in small batches. Return soup to pot and stir in olive oil, cumin, paprika, lemon juice, salt and pepper. Heat just to a boil and serve at once.

TUSCAN BEAN SOUP AU GRATIN

Servings: 6-8

This soup is a wonderful company dish for a cold winter evening.

2½ cups small white beans
2-3 tbs. olive oil
1 clove garlic, minced
1 onion, chopped
1 carrot, peeled, chopped
1 stalk celery, chopped
2 leeks, white and some green, sliced
1 sprig rosemary
1 ham bone
salt and pepper

GARNISH

¾ cup extra virgin olive oil
2 cloves garlic, minced
pinch of thyme
8 slices Italian bread, toasted
¾ cup freshly grated Parmesan cheese
1 onion, thinly sliced

Soak beans in water to cover overnight. Drain. Heat oil in a large soup pot and sauté garlic, onion, carrot, celery, leeks and rosemary until they begin to brown. Add beans and ham bone. Cover with water and simmer for 2 hours. Remove bone. Puree half the bean mixture in the blender in small batches. Add salt and pepper to taste. Return puree to pot.

For garnish: Heat olive oil and sauté garlic and thyme until garlic is golden. Discard garlic and pour half the oil into soup. Stir well. Arrange slices of toast in the bottom of an ovenproof tureen or casserole and sprinkle with half the cheese. Pour soup over toast and cheese. Cover with sliced onion and add remaining oil and cheese. Bake at 375° for 30 minutes. Serve from the tureen.

GARBANZO VELVET SOUP

Servings: 4

Garbanzo beans, also known as chick peas, date to Neolithic times and were introduced to the New World by the Spaniards in the sixteenth century. Onion, lemon and cumin are time-tested companions.

1 onion, chopped
1 clove garlic, minced
1 tbs. canola oil
1 can (15 oz.) garbanzo beans, with liquid
2 cups water
1 tsp. cumin
1 tbs. lemon juice
salt and pepper
1/4 cup chopped cilantro for garnish

Sauté onion and garlic in oil until soft. Add beans and their liquid, water, cumin and lemon juice. Simmer for 10 minutes. Puree in the blender in small batches. Add salt and pepper to taste, garnish with chopped cilantro and serve at once.

FRESH TOMATO-WINE SOUP

Servings: 4

Serve this smooth soup piping hot. Its flavor is fresh and lovely — making it with really ripe tomatoes is important.

2 cups peeled, seeded, diced ripe tomatoes
4 tbs. butter
2 tbs. flour
$\frac{1}{8}$ tsp. freshly grated nutmeg
$\frac{1}{4}$ tsp. baking soda
1 cup half and half
$\frac{1}{2}$ cup dry white wine
salt and pepper

Simmer tomatoes in butter for 5 minutes. Puree in the blender and return puree to pot. Blend in flour and nutmeg with a whisk and bring mixture to a boil, stirring constantly. Simmer for 2 minutes. Whisk in soda, half and half and wine. Bring just to a boil, add salt and pepper to taste and serve at once.

CURRIED AVOCADO SOUP
WITH WHITE WINE

Servings: 6

Curry and avocados are a wonderful flavor combination and, if you've never experienced avocado soup, you are in for a treat. Try to use the dark-skinned Haas avocados for their superior flavor.

½ onion, minced
3 tbs. canola or avocado oil
3 tbs. flour
1 tbs. curry powder, or to taste
3 cups milk

3 ripe avocados, peeled, mashed
salt and pepper
½ cup dry white wine
chopped parsley or cilantro for garnish

Sauté onion in oil until soft. Add flour and curry powder and cook, stirring, for 3 minutes. Turn heat to low and gradually whisk in milk. Whisk and heat until it just reaches a boil. Remove from heat and stir in avocados, salt and pepper to taste and wine. Puree in small batches in the blender. Remove puree to a bowl and chill for at least 4 hours. Garnish with parsley or cilantro to serve.

CREAM OF WATERCRESS SOUP

Servings: 6

Called Creme de Cresson in French, this soup is a delightful way to start a meal.

2 bunches watercress
8 cups chicken stock

salt and pepper
1 cup half and half

Wash cress and discard thick stems. Combine with stock and simmer for 5 minutes. Puree in the blender in small batches. Return puree to pot. Add salt and pepper to taste and whisk in half and half. Heat just to a boil and serve at once.

CUCUMBER SOUP

Servings: 4

For years this was the summer soup of choice in our family. Make it early in the day and have it nicely chilled for dinner. Don't worry too much about exact amounts.

2 large cucumbers, peeled, seeded, chopped
1 large onion, chopped
generous pinch of dill weed

6 cups chicken stock
1 cup sour cream or plain yogurt
fresh dill weed for garnish

Simmer cucumbers, onion and dill in stock until vegetables are very soft. Puree in blender in small batches. Pour puree into a bowl and whisk in sour cream or yogurt. Chill thoroughly. Garnish each serving with a sprig or fresh dill.

SPLIT PEA AND FRESH PEA SOUP

Servings: 4

This soup is a lovely green color and the flavor of both the fresh (or frozen) and the dried split peas comes through.

1 cup green split peas
4 cups chicken stock
1/2 stalk celery, sliced
1/2 onion, chopped
1/2 carrot, peeled, sliced
1 lb. fresh peas or 8 oz. frozen tiny peas

1/2 bay leaf
1 sprig thyme or 1/4 tsp. dried
salt and pepper
1 cup half and half
1-2 tbs. butter, optional

Place split peas in a pot with stock, celery, onion and carrot and simmer until peas are tender, 1 1/2 to 2 hours. If using fresh peas, shell them, steam until just tender and add to cooked mixture. If using frozen peas, defrost and add to cooked mixture. Puree in the blender in small batches. Return puree to pot. Add bay leaf, thyme, salt and pepper to taste; simmer for 10 minutes. Just before serving, stir in half and half and heat just to a boil. Swirl in a chunk of butter, if desired.

CREAM OF BUCKWHEAT SOUP

Servings: 4

This most unusual soup is especially hearty and delicious on a cold evening. Buckwheat groats, often called kasha, are sold in supermarkets and health food stores.

½ cup buckwheat groats
1 egg, lightly beaten
¾ cup chopped onion
2 tbs. butter
3 cups chicken stock
¼ lb. spinach, washed, stemmed
¼ tsp. freshly grated nutmeg
2 cups half and half
salt and pepper

Combine buckwheat and egg and cook, stirring, over medium heat until grains separate. Set aside. Sauté onion in butter for 3 minutes and add to buckwheat. Add stock, spinach and nutmeg and simmer, covered, for 15 minutes or until the buckwheat is tender. Puree in the blender in small batches. Return to pot and stir in half and half. Add salt and pepper to taste and serve hot.

CREAM OF SPINACH SOUP

Servings: 4

This attractive and easy-to-prepare soup is a favorite in Sweden where it comes to the table in flat soup plates with a half deviled egg gracing each serving.

1 lb. fresh spinach, large stems
  removed
3 tbs. butter
2 tbs. flour
1 cup milk
1½ cups beef broth

1 cup half and half
1 tsp. lemon juice
salt and pepper
2 deviled eggs (4 halves)
freshly grated nutmeg

Sauté spinach in butter until it is wilted. Sprinkle with flour and stir and cook 2 minutes. Add milk and broth and simmer 20 minutes. Puree in the blender in small batches. Return puree to pot. Add half and half, lemon juice and salt and pepper to taste.

To serve: Ladle soup into 4 flat soup plates. Place half a deviled egg in each plate and dust with nutmeg. Serve at once.

FRENCH MUSHROOM SOUP

Servings: 4

This Provençal-style mushroom soup is delicious hot or cold.

2 slices firm-textured white bread
3½ cups chicken stock
¾ lb. mushrooms, cleaned, chopped
2 tbs. butter
1 clove garlic, minced
1 tsp. minced parsley
¼ tsp. freshly grated nutmeg
½ cup heavy cream
salt and pepper

Soak bread in stock and set aside. Sauté mushrooms in butter for 2 minutes. Add garlic, parsley and nutmeg; simmer for 5 minutes. Squeeze stock from bread and stir bread into mushroom mixture. Mix thoroughly. Add stock and simmer for 10 minutes. Puree in the blender in small batches. Return puree to pot. Bring just to a boil. Add cream and stir well. Add salt and pepper to taste and serve at once.

CREME ST. JACQUES

Servings: 4

This wonderfully elegant soup makes one cup of scallops go a long way.

3 cups water
2 potatoes, peeled, quartered
1 onion, chopped
1 clove garlic, minced
½ bay leaf
¼ tsp. thyme
1 cup scallops, coarsely chopped
1 egg yolk
⅓ cup heavy cream or half and half
salt and pepper

Bring water to a boil. Add potatoes, onion, garlic, bay leaf and thyme. Simmer 30 minutes. Add scallops and simmer 5 minutes. Remove bay leaf. Puree in the blender in small batches. Return puree to pot and bring just to a boil. Remove from heat. Mix together egg yolk and half and half; whisk into soup. Serve at once.

DAVID'S PEANUT SOUP

This soup, with its West African overtones, is luscious and creamy. It's also quite rich and best served in small portions.

2 cups sliced onions
2 tbs. butter or canola oil
2 carrots, peeled, cut into pieces
2 stalks celery, cut into pieces
6 cups chicken stock
1 cup peanut butter, smooth or chunky
salt and pepper

Sauté onions in butter until soft. Add carrots, celery and stock and simmer until vegetables are very tender. Puree in the blender in small batches. Return puree to pot and whisk in peanut butter. Add more stock, if necessary. Add salt and pepper to taste and serve very hot.

ZUCCHINI SOUP

Servings: 4

For all zucchini lovers, a delicate, sophisticated and delicious soup.

1 onion, chopped
1 clove garlic, minced
4 tbs. butter or canola oil
3 cups sliced zucchini
4 cups chicken stock
1/4 tsp. finely minced rosemary
1 tbs. lemon juice

1/2 cup dry white wine
4 tbs. dry Madeira or sherry
3/4 cup grated Swiss cheese
salt and pepper
1/2 cup finely chopped zucchini for garnish

Sauté onion and garlic in butter or oil until soft but not brown. Add sliced zucchini. Cook and stir for 5 minutes. Add stock, rosemary, lemon juice and white wine; simmer for 20 minutes. Puree in the blender in small batches. Return puree to pot and add Madeira and grated cheese. Simmer until bubbly. Add salt and pepper to taste and serve at once garnished with finely chopped raw zucchini.

MEXICAN CORN SOUP

Servings: 6

This "full meal soup" can be made with either fresh or frozen corn kernels.

3½ cups corn kernels (8 -12 ears)
1 cup chicken stock
4 tbs. butter
2 cups milk
1 clove garlic, minced
1 tsp. oregano
salt and pepper
1-2 tbs. canned green chilies, rinsed,
  diced, or 1-2 jalapeños, seeded,
  minced

1 whole cooked chicken breast, boned,
  chopped, optional
1 cup peeled, seeded, diced tomatoes
1 cup cubed Monterey Jack cheese
2 tbs. minced parsley or cilantro
tortilla chips

In small batches, puree corn with chicken stock in the blender. Melt butter in a large soup pot and add corn puree. Simmer and stir over low heat for 5 minutes. Add milk, garlic, oregano, and salt and pepper to taste. Bring to a boil. Reduce heat, add chilies and simmer for 5 minutes. Divide chicken and tomatoes among 6 soup bowls. Remove soup from heat. Add cheese and stir until just melted. Ladle soup into bowls and top with parsley or cilantro and tortilla chips. Serve at once.

CHILLED PIMIENTO SOUP

Use pimientos that come packed in jars or, when they are available fresh in the fall, roast your own. Either way, this unusual soup is a fine way to begin a meal of grilled meat or fish.

1/2 onion, chopped
2 tbs. canola oil
2 tbs. flour
2 1/2 cups chicken stock, all fat removed
1 jar (4 oz.) whole pimientos, or 3 fresh pimientos, roasted, peeled
1 cup half and half
salt and pepper
dill weed for garnish

Sauté onions in oil until soft. Sprinkle with flour and cook-stir for 1 minute. Slowly add stock and cook 5 minutes. Remove seeds from pimientos, either canned or fresh roasted, and place them in the blender. Add soup, in several batches if necessary, and puree. Remove puree to a bowl and stir in half and half. Add salt and pepper to taste and chill for several hours. Garnish with dill weed at serving time.

GAZPACHO

Gazpacho recipes are legion. This one has been my summer favorite for many years.

4 cloves garlic
½ onion, chopped
1 bunch green onions, chopped
2 green bell peppers, seeded, chopped

2 large cucumbers, peeled, seeded, chopped
1 tbs. sugar
6 cups chicken stock

Puree all ingredients in the blender in small batches, dividing liquid among batches equally. Remove puree to a large bowl and add:

1 can (28 oz.) chopped tomatoes
1 can (28 oz.) ground tomatoes
3-4 cups chicken stock
olive oil, white wine vinegar, Tabasco
  Sauce and salt to taste

¾ cup dry bread crumbs
1 cucumber, peeled, seeded, finely chopped

Correct seasonings and chill thoroughly.

SOPA DE QUESO

Servings: 4

When you're in the mood for a South-of-the-Border flavor trip, this soup will speed you on your way.

½ large onion, chopped
4 tbs. butter or canola oil
2 large tomatoes, peeled, seeded, chopped
1 can (4 oz.) whole green chilies, seeded
salt
dash of cumin
2 cups chicken stock
1 cup grated Monterey Jack cheese
avocado slices and/or tortilla chips for garnish

Sauté onion in butter until soft. In the blender, puree onion, tomatoes, chilies, salt, cumin and chicken stock in small batches. Remove puree to pot. Heat over low heat but do not allow to boil. Gradually add cheese and stir until soup reaches a smooth consistency. Serve at once garnished with avocado slices and/or tortilla chips.

CHILLED MULLIGATAWNY SOUP

Servings: 8

I've never served this soup to other than rave reviews. Its exotic goodness depends on fully ripe mangos.

4 onions, minced
½ cup canola oil
2 cloves garlic, minced
4 tsp. peeled, minced fresh ginger root
1 tbs. curry powder
1 tbs. ground coriander
2 tsp. cumin
¼ tsp. turmeric

¼ tsp. cayenne
4 cups chicken stock
3 carrots, peeled, thinly sliced
1 cup peeled, diced mango
¼ cup minced parsley
1 can (14 oz.) coconut milk
salt and pepper
half and half to thin, if necessary

Sauté onions in oil until soft. Add garlic and ginger and cook 2 minutes. Add curry powder, coriander, cumin, turmeric and cayenne. Stir and cook for 1 minute. Add chicken stock, carrots, mango and parsley. Bring to a boil, reduce heat and simmer for 45 minutes. Stir occasionally. Puree in small batches in the blender. Return puree to pot. Stir in coconut milk, bring to a boil, reduce heat and simmer 3 minutes. Add salt and pepper to taste. Cool; refrigerate for at least 4 hours. This makes a very thick puree and may need thinning with a little half and half.

PUMPKIN VEGETABLE SOUP

Servings: 6

Simple to prepare, smooth and creamy, this soup is perfect for a crisp autumn day.

1 cup minced onion
1 stalk celery, cut into pieces
1 carrot, peeled, cut into pieces
4 tbs. canola oil
2 cups cooked pumpkin (canned is OK)

2 cups chicken stock
1½ cups half and half
⅔ cup fresh squeezed orange juice
salt and pepper

GARNISH
1 cup sour cream or plain yogurt
1 tsp. minced chives

2 tsp. grated orange peel

Sauté onions, celery and carrot in oil for 10 minutes. Stir in pumpkin and chicken stock and simmer for 15 minutes. Puree in blender in small batches. Return puree to pot. Stir in half and half, orange juice and salt and pepper to taste. Simmer for 10 minutes. Combine sour cream, chives and orange peel. Add a dollop to each serving.

LINDA'S SORREL SOUP

Servings: 6

My daughter-in-law, Linda, grows her own sorrel for this sumptuous cold soup, but that is not a necessary step. On a hot summer evening, this is a perfect meal starter.

2 large onions, thinly sliced
5 cloves garlic, minced
4 tbs. canola oil
12 oz. or about 10 cups fresh sorrel
  leaves, stems removed

4 cups chicken stock
1/2 cup minced parsley
salt and pepper
pinch of cayenne

GARNISH

1 cup sour cream or plain yogurt
minced chives

nasturtium blossoms, optional

Sauté onions and garlic in oil until soft. Add sorrel. Cover pot and cook until sorrel is wilted, about 5 minutes. Add stock, parsley, salt, pepper and cayenne and bring to a boil. Reduce heat and simmer for 45 minutes. Puree soup in the blender in small batches. Remove puree to a bowl and chill at least 4 hours. Garnish each serving with a dollop of sour cream or yogurt, a sprinkling of chives and a nasturtium blossom.

CARROT-APPLE SOUP

Servings: 6

When I make this luscious soup, I use frozen concentrated Granny Smith apple juice which has no added sugar and a good clean taste. Serve it either hot or cold. It's a great treat for breakfast or brunch.

1 lb. carrots, peeled, cut into pieces
6 cups cider or apple juice
3 large tart apples, peeled, cored, chopped
1 small onion, chopped
3 tbs. canola oil
2 tbs. brandy, optional

¼ cup brown sugar
½ tsp. freshly grated nutmeg
½ tsp. cinnamon
¼ tsp. ground ginger
plain yogurt and raisins, for garnish, optional

Combine carrots and cider and bring to a boil. Reduce heat and simmer until carrots are very tender. Sauté apples and onion in oil until soft. Add brandy, sugar, nutmeg, cinnamon and ginger; combine with carrots. Puree in the blender in small batches. Remove puree to a bowl and chill at least 4 hours or serve hot. Garnish with yogurt and raisins, if desired.

CHILLED MELON SOUP

Servings: 6-8

This is my favorite soup to start a summer brunch or dinner. To be especially festive, serve the soup in long-stemmed wine glasses.

3 cups cantaloupe, coarsely chopped
3 cups honeydew, coarsely chopped
2 cups fresh squeezed orange juice
⅓ cup fresh squeezed lime juice
3 tbs. honey, or to taste (depends on the melons)
2 cups dry white wine
mint leaves for garnish

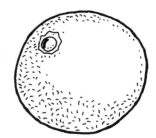

Finely chop 1½ cups each of cantaloupe and honeydew and set aside. Puree remaining melon in the blender in small batches with orange juice, lime juice and honey. Remove puree to a bowl and stir in wine and reserved melon. Chill at least 4 hours. Serve in large glasses garnished with mint leaves.

SAUCES, SWEET AND SAVORY

LEMON OR ORANGE SAUCE

Yield: 1½ cups

This flavorful sauce is perfect with warm gingerbread or with any simple cake.

2 egg yolks
1 cup water
¾ cup sugar
2 tbs. cornstarch
pinch of salt
1 whole lemon, peeled, seeded, or ½ orange, peeled, seeded
peel of ½ lemon or ½ orange, cut into pieces

Place all ingredients in the blender and process until smooth. Transfer to a saucepan and cook over low heat, stirring constantly, until thick.

RASPBERRY OR STRAWBERRY SAUCE

Yield: 1½ cups

This simple sauce is luscious over ice cream, but you will probably find many other uses for it as well.

1 pkg. (12 oz.) frozen, unsweetened raspberries or strawberries

3 tbs. red currant jelly
2 tbs. confectioners' sugar

Thaw berries and puree in the blender. If using raspberries, press through a sieve to remove seeds. Melt jelly over low heat, stirring until smooth. Whisk jelly and sugar into berry puree. Refrigerate.

BRANDY HARD SAUCE

Yield: about 1¼ cups

This traditional sauce is wonderful to have on hand in the refrigerator. It's especially good with warm steamed puddings, mince pies and gingerbread.

⅓ cup soft butter
1 egg yolk
2 tbs. brandy

2½ cups confectioners' sugar

Place all ingredients in the blender and process until smooth. Store in the refrigerator, but bring to room temperature to serve.

BASIC MAYONNAISE

Yield: about 1 cup

This extremely simple-to-make, basic mayonnaise tastes so fresh and good that you'll probably not be tempted to return to the commercial variety. TIP: If your mayonnaise should curdle, (not a common occurrence) remove it from the blender and set aside. Wash and dry the blender container and add one whole egg. With the motor running, gradually add the curdled mayonnaise. Blend until smooth.

1 whole egg or 2 egg yolks
2 tbs. lemon juice or vinegar
1/4 tsp. salt

1/2 tsp. dry mustard
1 cup canola oil

Place egg, lemon juice, salt, mustard and 1/4 cup of oil in the blender. Begin to blend and, with motor running, add remaining oil in a slow, steady stream until proper consistency is reached. Refrigerate.

MAYONNAISE VARIATIONS

- Use different vinegars (fruit, sherry, rice) and different oils (olive, nut) to change the flavor of a basic mayonnaise. A full-flavored oil is generally best used in combination with another less assertive one.

- **Roasted Garlic Mayonnaise:** Incorporate 2 heads of roasted garlic (see page 7) which have been pressed from the skins and additional lemon juice to taste.

- **Herb Mayonnaise:** Add fresh or dried herbs to taste. Herbs such as parsley and cilantro can be used in amounts up to ½ cup.

- **Curry Mayonnaise:** Add 1 tbs. curry powder (or to taste), 2 tbs. tomato paste, 2 green onions, cut into pieces and 1 clove of garlic, cut into pieces to basic mayonnaise and blend well before adding oil.

- **Mango Mayonnaise:** Cut flesh of a peeled, fully ripe mango into small pieces and add to basic recipe before adding oil. Omit dry mustard.

- **Chipolte Mayonnaise:** Add 2 canned chipolte chilies (in adobo sauce) and 2 tbs. of the sauce to basic recipe before adding oil. Omit dry mustard and finish mayonnaise with 1 tsp. balsamic vinegar, if desired.

- **Ancho Chili Mayonnaise:** Heat 1½ cups water to a boil and add 1 ancho chili, stemmed and seeded. Soak for 25 minutes. Peel off and discard skin and add pulp to the blender along with 1 jalapeño, stemmed and seeded, 2 cloves garlic, peeled and 2 whole eggs plus the usual amounts of lemon juice, dry mustard and salt. Slightly more oil may be needed to create the proper consistency. Several sprigs of cilantro may be added, if desired.

HOLLANDAISE SAUCE

Hollandaise sauce is nothing to fear. In fact, it's quick and easy and almost foolproof with the blender to help you.

½ cup butter
3 egg yolks
1 tbs. lemon juice
dash of Tabasco Sauce or pinch of cayenne

Heat butter in a saucepan until very hot. Be careful not to brown. Place remaining ingredients in the blender and pulse to combine. With motor running, add melted butter in a steady stream until sauce is emulsified and smooth. The finished sauce may be kept warm over hot water in a bowl.

HOLLANDAISE VARIATIONS

- Add 1-2 tbs. minced fresh herbs after the butter. Parsley, cilantro, rosemary and sage all work well (not together, though), depending on what the sauce is to be served with.
- Add up to 2 tbs. minced, roasted chili peppers after the butter.

BLENDER WHITE SAUCE

Yield: about 1 cup

With this method, the sauce is guaranteed to have no lumps.

1½ tbs. butter, softened
1½ tbs. flour
1 cup milk or half and half

Place all ingredients in the blender and process until completely smooth. Transfer to a saucepan and cook over low heat, stirring constantly until thickened. Season with salt and pepper.

VARIATION

- **Cheese Sauce:** Add ½ cup cheese, cut in cubes, before blending.

BASIL CREAM SAUCE

Yield: about 2 cups

This wonderfully aromatic sauce takes full advantage of fresh basil and should be reserved for a time when it is available. It is delicious on pasta, salads and cooked vegetables.

½ cup heavy cream
2 tbs. Dijon mustard
¾ cup tightly packed fresh basil leaves, cut into pieces
1-2 large cloves garlic
⅓ cup canola oil
1 cup sour cream
salt

Place cream, mustard, basil leaves and garlic in the blender and puree until almost smooth. With motor running, slowly add oil and puree until completely smooth. Transfer to a bowl and stir in sour cream and salt to taste. Refrigerate for several hours, but bring to room temperature before serving.

TOMATO SAUCE

Yield: about 2 cups

It's easy to make an excellent tomato sauce with just the ingredients you like best. The secret is to use very good quality tomatoes. Use this as a basic recipe and vary it according to your taste.

1 can (28 oz.) Italian tomatoes with liquid
1 large onion, cut into pieces
2-3 cloves garlic, cut into pieces
1-2 sprigs fresh basil
2 tbs. red wine or red wine vinegar
½ tbs. sugar
2 tbs. olive oil
1 bay leaf
salt and pepper

Place tomatoes with liquid, onion, garlic, basil and vinegar in the blender and process until as smooth as desired. Transfer to a saucepan. Add sugar, olive oil, bay leaf and salt and pepper to taste. Simmer for 10 minutes or longer to reach desired thickness.

MEXICAN SALSA

Yield: about 1½ cups

Depending on how many chili peppers you include, this salsa will be as hot or mild as you choose. The number will not affect the proportions of the other ingredients.

2-6 jalapeños, cut into pieces
1-2 cloves garlic, cut into pieces
½ medium onion, cut into pieces
10-12 sprigs cilantro
1 can (14 oz.) Italian tomatoes, drained
1 tsp. lemon juice
salt and pepper

Place all ingredients except salt and pepper in the blender and process to desired consistency. (It is best to leave some chunks.) Add salt and pepper to taste.

CUMIN-CORIANDER INDIAN RAITA

Yield: about 2½ cups

Raitas are classic Indian sauces, served with hot spicy curries to tame the fire. The first is good with broiled or grilled chicken and fish as well as with curries. The variation is the perfect addition to meat or vegetarian pita sandwiches.

1½ cups plain yogurt
1 tsp. salt
3 tbs. cilantro leaves

½ tsp. cumin
1 small cucumber, peeled, seeded, chopped

Combine yogurt, salt, cilantro and cumin in the blender until cilantro is coarsely chopped. Transfer to a bowl and stir in cucumber. Chill before serving.

RAITA VARIATION

Yield: about 2½ cups

1 cup plain yogurt
½ onion, cut into pieces
1 tomato, peeled, seeded, cut into pieces
¼ tsp. cumin

¼ tsp. salt
2 tbs. cilantro leaves
1 small cucumber, peeled, chopped

Combine all ingredients except cucumber and process in the blender until all ingredients are coarsely chopped. Transfer to a bowl and stir in cucumber. Chill before serving.

RED PEPPER SAUCE

Robust and sweet, Red Pepper Sauce is perfect on a salad or first course of avocados, shrimp and thinly sliced cucumbers. You'll find many other uses as well — including as a sauce for pasta.

¾ lb. red bell peppers, roasted (see page 7)
1 tbs. olive oil, or to taste
dash of Tabasco Sauce
salt and pepper

Peel roasted peppers and discard stems and seeds. Place in the blender with olive oil and Tabasco; blend to a smooth puree. Add salt and pepper to taste. Serve at room temperature.

TUNA MAYONNAISE FOR PASTA

Yield: about 1½ cups

This light and delicious sauce for pasta is also an unusual partner with cold chicken, hard boiled eggs and raw vegetables.

2 tbs. capers, well drained
12 black olives, pitted
8 tbs. mayonnaise
4 tbs. lemon juice
1 can (10 oz.) water-packed tuna, well drained and flaked
2 tbs. parsley

Chop capers and slice olives; set aside. Place mayonnaise, lemon juice, tuna and parsley in the blender and blend to a smooth puree. Transfer to a bowl and stir in capers and olives.

RED PEPPER AND GARLIC BUTTER

Yield: about 2 cups

Every time I make this pasta sauce, I say the same thing — it's fabulous!

2 red bell peppers, roasted (see page 7)
4 cloves garlic
1/4 lb. butter, very soft, cut into pieces
2 tbs. olive oil
1 tsp. salt
1 tsp. hot water
nutmeg
pepper

Remove stems and seeds from peppers. Poach whole, unpeeled garlic cloves in water to cover for 5 minutes. Drain and peel. Place peppers, garlic, butter, olive oil and salt in the blender and blend to a smooth puree. With motor running, add hot water. Transfer to a bowl and add freshly grated nutmeg and pepper to taste.

RED PEPPER-ONION SAUCE

Yield: about 2 cups

Roasted peppers and long, slow cooking give this beautiful pasta sauce its wonderful depth of flavor. It's worth the time it takes. Top the finished dish with freshly grated grated Parmesan cheese.

4 red bell peppers, roasted (see page 7)
2 medium onions, sliced very thin
4 tbs. butter
1/3 cup dry white wine

Remove stems and seeds from peppers. Cut into thin strips and reserve any juice. Sauté onions in butter over low heat, stirring occasionally, for about 1 hour or until soft and golden. Add wine and peppers, with any juice, to onions and continue cooking until mixture is thick and syrupy, about 5 to 10 minutes. Place 1/3 of the mixture in the blender and puree. Transfer to a bowl and stir in remaining 2/3. If sauce is too thick, add a little hot water.

LEMON-DILL BUTTER

Yield: ½ cup

This is wonderful on hot fish, shrimp or scallops.

8 tbs. very soft butter
1 tsp. dill weed

1 tsp. lemon juice
salt and pepper

Place butter, dill and lemon juice in the blender and process until smooth. Add salt and pepper to taste. Refrigerate until ready to use.

CHUTNEY-ORANGE BUTTER

Yield: ¾ cup

Savory butters are great for sandwiches and also on bread and crackers served with soup or salad.

8 tbs. very soft butter
3 tbs. chutney
1½ tsp. grated orange peel

1 tsp. orange juice
8 walnut halves

Combine all ingredients in the blender and process to a coarse puree. It is best if not too smooth, as some texture makes it more interesting.

SALSA VERDE

Yield: about 2 cups

Originally, this sauce was served with the classic Italian dish, bolito misti (mixed boiled meats). It is, however, equally delicious on pasta or as a dipping sauce for raw vegetables. To cure the raw taste, it needs time to age, so make it early in the day or the day before.

1 bunch parsley, preferably flat leaf Italian
1 tsp. capers, drained
2-3 anchovy fillets, optional
2-3 sweet gherkins
2 cloves garlic, cut into pieces
1 green onion
2 slices firm white bread, soaked in water, squeezed dry
½ cup olive oil
salt and pepper

Place all ingredients except olive oil, salt and pepper in the blender. In small batches, process to a smooth consistency. Transfer to a bowl and whisk in olive oil. Add salt and pepper to taste. Refrigerate for several hours. Bring to room temperature to serve.

WALNUT SAUCE

This sauce is bright green. Try it for St. Patrick's Day. The flavor is mild, but rich and smooth. It's delicious on fish or steamed vegetables as well as on freshly cooked hot pasta.

¼ cup shelled walnuts
1 bunch parsley, preferably flat leaf Italian
2 tbs. dry bread crumbs
1 cup oil, preferably walnut oil
2-4 tbs. heavy cream
salt and pepper

Puree walnuts in the blender. Add parsley and bread crumbs and, with motor running, gradually add oil until a thick paste is formed. Transfer to a bowl and stir in cream to desired consistency. Add salt and pepper to taste.

GARLIC-HERB SAUCE

Yield: about ¾ cup

This simple and delicious sauce is the creation of San Francisco chef Robert Reynolds. It's wonderful with roast lamb or chicken.

2 heads of garlic, peeled
chicken stock
several sprigs fresh herbs (thyme, rosemary, mint, cilantro — whatever is
  compatible with your entrée)
1 tbs. butter
salt and pepper

In a small saucepan, simmer garlic in stock to cover for 30 minutes. Place garlic and stock in the blender with the herb of choice and blend to a smooth puree. Transfer to a bowl and, while still hot, stir in butter. Season to taste with salt and pepper.

SKORDALIA

This time-tested Greek sauce is as versatile as it is delicious. Use it on pasta, over cold fish, with steamed vegetables, or on sautéed eggplant and zucchini. It's especially good with artichokes.

⅓ cup toasted walnuts
4 cloves garlic, peeled, blanched in boiling water for 1 minute
1 egg
½ tsp. grated lemon peel
½ cup olive oil
½ cup canola oil
1 tbs. white wine vinegar
2 tbs. lemon juice
salt

Put nuts in the blender and process to a fine meal. Remove and set aside. Put garlic, egg and lemon peel in blender and pulse a few times. With motor running, slowly add half the oil. Scrape down sides. Add vinegar, lemon juice and remaining oil. Blend until sauce thickens. Transfer to a bowl and stir in walnuts. Add salt to taste. Refrigerate for several hours or overnight but bring to room temperature to serve.

BATTERS

BLENDER POPOVERS

Yield: 8-10

With the blender, these spectacular treats couldn't be easier.

2 eggs
1 cup milk
1 cup flour
pinch of salt
1 tbs. melted butter, optional

Preheat oven to 450°. Butter and heat a muffin tin. Combine all ingredients in the blender and process until smooth. Pour batter into hot muffin cups, filling half way. Bake at 450° for 10 minutes. Reduce heat to 350° and continue baking for 35 minutes or until popovers are puffed and golden. Remove from tin and serve at once.

GARLIC POPOVERS

These savory popovers are perfect for lunch or supper with a bowl of chili or soup.

butter
4 eggs
1 cup milk
1 cup flour
1 tsp. salt
¼ tsp. baking powder
2 tsp. finely crushed Herbs de Provence
12-14 cloves roasted garlic (see page 7)

Place ½ tsp. butter in each muffin tin and heat in a 450° oven for 5 minutes. Combine eggs and milk in the blender. With the motor running, add dry ingredients and blend thoroughly. Transfer batter to a bowl. Squeeze roasted garlic into batter and stir to combine. Pour into hot muffin tins, filling them ⅔ full. Bake at 450° for 20 minutes. If tops are not brown and firm, bake 5 minutes longer.

FRESH CORN POPOVERS

Yield: 6

Bake these irresistible popovers in large custard cups or in large muffin tins. If made in advance, the batter can rest, covered, at room temperature for up to 2 hours.

⅓ cup fresh corn kernels
⅓ cup water
2 eggs
½ cup milk

1 tbs. corn or canola oil
½ tsp. salt
white pepper
1 cup flour

Heat oven to 425°. Generously oil custard cups (placed on a baking sheet) or muffin tins. Heat in oven until very hot, about 4 minutes. Place corn kernels and water in the blender and process until corn is finely chopped. Drain through a sieve into a measuring cup. Add more water, if necessary, to make ½ cup liquid. Reserve chopped corn. In blender, combine corn liquid, eggs, milk, corn oil, salt and pepper until well blended. With the motor running, add flour and combine thoroughly. Transfer batter to a bowl and stir in corn. Ladle ⅓ cup batter into each hot custard cup.

Bake at 425° for 15 minutes. Reduce heat to 400° and bake until popovers are firm and browned, about 20 minutes. Remove from oven and carefully pierce one side of each popover just above the cup rim with the tip of a sharp knife. Remove popovers from cups and place on their sides on baking sheet. Bake another 5 minutes and serve immediately.

COTTAGE CHEESE PANCAKES

These flavorful pancakes are delicate, moist and light.

2 cups cottage cheese
6 eggs
½ cup flour

Place cottage cheese and eggs in the blender and process until smooth. With the motor running, add flour. Scrape down sides as necessary to blend and combine thoroughly. Drop batter by spoonfuls on a lightly buttered griddle or skillet. When underside is brown and top side is dry, turn and brown second side. Serve hot with syrup or jam.

THE PANCAKE

Every book that includes breakfast recipes inevitably lists this recipe or one that is similar. Since it is perfectly suited to the blender, I include it, too. It goes by many names — Dutch Baby, German or Oven Baked Pancake. In our house we simply call it THE Pancake and we enjoy it often.

2 tbs. unsalted butter
1 egg
¼ cup milk
½ tsp. vanilla
¼ cup flour

Preheat oven to 475°. Put butter in an individual baking dish or ramekin and heat in oven until melted. Place egg, milk and vanilla in the blender and blend thoroughly. With motor running, add flour. Scrape down sides as necessary. Pour batter into melted butter in baking dish and return dish to oven. Bake until pancake is puffed and golden, about 10 or 15 minutes. Remove from baking dish and serve at once with sautéed or sliced fresh fruit or simply drizzled with lemon juice and dusted with confectioners' sugar.

SAVORY CHEESE PANCAKES

These are great for breakfast or a quick snack.

2 eggs
2 tbs. milk
2 tbs. sharp cheddar cheese, diced
1 green onion, cut into pieces
½ tsp. jalapeño, seeded, minced
1 tbs. melted butter
salt and pepper

Place all ingredients in the blender and process until smooth. Drop by spoonfuls onto a lightly greased, hot griddle or skillet and cook until brown on the bottom and dry on top. Turn and brown second side.

EASY CORNMEAL PANCAKES

Servings: 4

Be traditional and serve these crispy pancakes with butter and syrup or be adventurous and serve them with salsa and sour cream.

1¼ cups buttermilk
1 egg
1 cup cornmeal
½ tsp. baking soda
½ tsp. salt

Place all ingredients in the blender and process until smooth. Drop by spoonfuls onto a hot, lightly greased griddle or skillet. Cook until brown on the bottom and dry on top. Turn to brown on the second side.

BUTTERMILK PANCAKES

This quick breakfast treat never fails to satisfy.

1 cup buttermilk
1 egg
1 tbs. sugar
1 cup flour
1 tsp. baking soda
pinch of salt
1 tbs. melted butter

Place all ingredients in the blender and process until smooth. Pour by spoonfuls onto a lightly greased griddle or skillet and cook until pancakes are browned on the bottom and dry on top. Turn to brown second side.

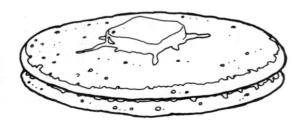

PEACH PANCAKE

This is wonderful with fresh, juicy peaches (peeled and pitted) or even with canned peach halves, well drained.

3 eggs
1½ cups milk
¾ cup flour
2 tbs. orange juice
salt
8 peach halves
confectioners' sugar

Preheat oven to 375°. Place eggs, milk, flour, orange juice and salt in the blender and process until smooth. Butter a deep, 8-inch diameter baking dish and pour in half the batter. Bake for 20 minutes. Remove from oven and arrange peach halves on top. Pour remaining batter over and return to oven. Bake an additional 25 minutes, or until batter has set. Serve immediately, dusted with confectioners' sugar.

BUCKWHEAT CREPES

Yield: twenty 5-inch crepes

These fragrant Old World crepes are tender and delicious and very versatile. Fill them, or simply top tiny ones with caviar and sour cream for an elegant appetizer or first course. Fill larger ones with meat filling (recipe follows) for an outstanding brunch or supper entrée.

¾ cup buckwheat flour
¼ cup whole wheat flour
¼ cup all purpose flour
3 eggs

1 cup milk
¼ cup water
½ tsp. salt
3 tbs. melted butter

Place all ingredients in the blender and process until thoroughly combined. Scrape down sides and blend for 2 minutes. Batter will be thin. Heat and butter a crepe pan. Pour a small amount of batter into pan and quickly tip pan to spread batter evenly. (The amount of batter for each crepe will depend on size of pan, but it should cover bottom of pan in a very thin layer.) As soon as top surface is covered with tiny bubbles, flip crepe and cook just long enough to dry second side. Remove to a plate.

RUSSIAN MEAT FILLING

½ cup minced onion
½ cup shredded green cabbage
3 tbs. butter
½ lb. ground chuck
2 hard boiled eggs, finely chopped

¼ cup minced fresh dill weed or 2 tsp. dried
¼ cup small curd cottage cheese or sour cream
salt and pepper

Sauté onion and cabbage in butter for 5 minutes. Add meat and continue to cook until meat is no longer pink. Stir in dill weed, eggs and cottage cheese. Remove from heat, add salt and pepper to taste and let mixture cool.

To assemble: Place several teaspoonfuls of filling on bottom third of each crepe. Roll loosely and place in a buttered baking dish, seam side down. Chill for 30 minutes. Brush rolled crepes with melted butter. Bake at 425° for 20 to 25 minutes. Serve with sour cream.

A note about pans: Special crepe pans are available in specialty cookware stores. Any small omelet-type pan with sloping sides will work well. Nonstick varieties are excellent and the heavier the pan, the better. Once the correct pan temperature is reached (medium-hot), the crepes cook quickly. Brush the pan lightly with melted butter for each crepe. Stack cooked crepes between paper towels.

FRESH CORN CREPES

Yield: twelve 6-inch crepes

Fill these tender crepes with chopped cooked chicken seasoned with chilies and cilantro for a brunch or supper treat. If made ahead, the batter can rest, covered, at room temperature for up to 2 hours or in the refrigerator for 6 hours. If it needs thinning, add milk 1 tablespoon at a time until the batter is the consistency of heavy cream.

3 large ears fresh sweet corn
3 tbs. cornstarch
¾ cup milk
2 eggs, lightly beaten
2½ tbs. butter, melted
salt

Blanch shucked corn ears in boiling water for 5 minutes. Drain and refresh under cold water. With a sharp knife, slice off kernels. Measure out 1 cup and puree in the blender. Add remaining ingredients and blend to combine thoroughly. Scrape down sides as necessary. Pour a small amount of batter into a heated and buttered crepe pan and cook until bottom is golden. Turn and cook until second side is dry. Stack cooked crepes between paper towels.

BASIC BLENDER WAFFLES

Yield: 6

Get all your ingredients out and have the waffle iron hot and ready. This recipe takes only seconds to prepare.

2 eggs
¼ cup canola oil or melted butter
1½ cups milk
1½ cups flour
2 tsp. baking powder
pinch of salt

Place all ingredients in the blender and process only until flour is completely moistened. Bake on a waffle iron according to the manufacturer's instructions.

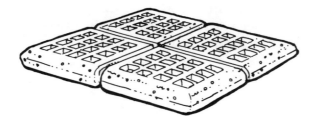

SOUR CREAM WAFFLES

Yield: 8

Any waffle lover will appreciate these rich, crispy breakfast treats.

3 eggs, separated
¾ cup milk
½ cup melted butter
¾ cup sour cream
1½ cups flour
½ tsp. baking soda
2 tsp. baking powder
1 tbs. sugar

Place egg yolks, milk, melted butter and sour cream in the blender and process until smooth. Combine flour, soda, baking powder and sugar. With motor running, add dry ingredients to mixture in blender. Combine until smooth and transfer to a large bowl. Beat egg whites to soft peaks and fold into batter. Bake on a waffle iron according to manufacturer's instructions.

BLUE CHEESE MUFFINS

Yield: 12

These savory muffins are an unusual breakfast treat.

2 cups flour
4 tsp. baking powder
1 tsp. sugar
1 egg
1 cup milk
3 tbs. soft butter
6 oz. blue cheese, crumbled

Preheat oven to 350° and butter muffin tins. Combine flour, baking powder and sugar in a bowl and set aside. Place egg, milk, butter and cheese in the blender and process until smooth. Pour into dry ingredients and mix just until flour is completely moistened. Fill muffin tins ⅔ full and bake for 30 minutes or until muffins test done.

ENTRÉES AND SIDE DISHES

GOAT CHEESE CUSTARDS

Servings: 6

I was completely captivated by these delicious savory custards served to me by a friend. They are good hot, at room temperature or cold. Fine as a first course served on a bed of lettuce, they are also good with roast chicken or meat.

1 cup half and half
3 eggs
6 oz. mild, creamy goat cheese, softened, cut into pieces
2 tsp. vanilla
2 tsp. fresh tarragon leaves
salt and pepper

Place half and half, eggs, cheese, vanilla and tarragon in the blender and process until smooth. Add salt and pepper to taste. Butter six ½-cup ramekins or custard cups and fill them with mixture. Place ramekins in a pan of hot water and bake at 350° for 30 minutes or until set.

BLUE CHEESE YOGURT MOLDS

Make these in ½-cup molds and serve them on a plate with a simple green salad.

1 envelope unflavored gelatin
½ cup water
2 oz. blue cheese, crumbled
2 cups plain yogurt
salt and pepper

In a saucepan, combine gelatin with water and stir over low heat until gelatin is dissolved. Transfer to the blender and add cheese and yogurt. Blend until smooth. Add salt and pepper to taste. Pour mixture into 6 small, lightly oiled ramekins or custard cups. Chill until firm. Unmold to serve.

COTTAGE CHEESE SOUFFLÉ

Servings: 6

This light luncheon or supper dish is simple to prepare. A hearty green salad is the perfect accompaniment.

6 eggs, separated
¼ cup skim milk
4 tsp. minced parsley
4 tbs. minced green onions
3 cups low fat cottage cheese
salt

Combine egg yolks, milk, parsley, green onions and cottage cheese in the blender and process until smooth. Add salt to taste. Transfer to a bowl. Beat egg whites until they hold soft peaks and fold them into cottage cheese mixture. Pour into a 1½- quart casserole or soufflé dish and bake at 300° for about 1 hour or until set. Serve at once.

MALFATTI

Servings: 6

Malfatti means misshaped in Italian. There is a story that long ago in Italy someone made ravioli and the little pasta packages lost their covers while cooking. What we have here is the delicious result!

1 pkg. (10 oz.) chopped frozen spinach
¼ loaf crusty French bread
½ onion, chopped
1 clove garlic, chopped
1 tbs. olive oil
2 eggs
¼ cup parsley
½ tsp. chopped basil leaves
½ cup grated Parmesan or dry Monterey Jack cheese
½ cup dry bread crumbs
salt and pepper
1½ cups tomato sauce

Cook spinach according to directions on package. Drain and squeeze dry. Cut French bread into chunks, soak in hot water and squeeze dry. Sauté onion and garlic in oil until soft. Combine with spinach and soaked bread. Stir in eggs, parsley and basil. In batches, blend mixture to a smooth puree in the blender. Transfer to a bowl and stir in ½ of the cheese and all bread crumbs. Add salt and pepper to taste.

With lightly floured hands, shape mixture into 2-inch "sausage" links. Drop links, a few at time, into a large pot of lightly salted, barely simmering water. Do not overcrowd. When malfatti rise to the top, remove with a slotted spoon and drain on paper towels. Place drained malfatti in a lightly oiled, shallow baking dish in 1 layer. Spoon tomato sauce over and sprinkle with remaining cheese. Reheat under the broiler.

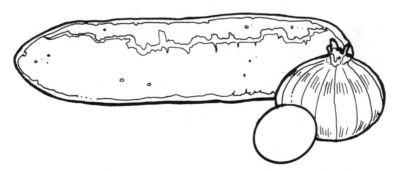

ONION TIMBALE

Servings: 4

This sweet onion custard is a great favorite. Serve it with chicken or broiled meat or as a separate course with tomato or cranberry coulis.

1½ lb. sliced onions
3 tbs. butter
1 cup water
2 cloves garlic, sliced
3 eggs
½ cup heavy cream
salt and pepper

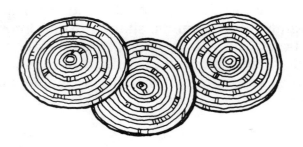

Sauté onions in butter until soft. Add water and garlic, cover and cook over medium heat for 5 minutes. Uncover and continue to cook until most of the water is absorbed. Spoon into the blender container and puree until smooth. With motor running, add eggs and heavy cream. Blend until smooth. Add salt and pepper to taste. Pour into 4 individual buttered ramekins. Place them in a pan of hot water and bake at 350° for 30 minutes or until custard is set. Cool 5 minutes. Run a knife around the edge and unmold.

MEAT LOAF

Servings: 8

Meat loaf is popular again. You may use this as a basic recipe and add your own spices, herbs and favorite touches, but it's quite good as given.

2 slices bread
1½ lb. ground beef
½ lb. ground pork
1 egg
½ cup canned tomatoes
2 tbs. catsup or salsa
1 onion, cut into pieces
2 stalks celery, with leaves, cut up
¼ cup parsley
2 tsp. salt
½ tsp. pepper

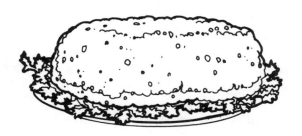

Tear bread into pieces and process into crumbs in blender. Add them to meat in a bowl. Place remaining ingredients in the blender and blend until vegetables are coarsely chopped. Pour this mixture over meat and crumbs and mix well. Pack into a meat loaf pan or form into a loaf and place on a pie plate. Bake at 350° for about 1 hour.

CURRIED CHICKEN MOLD

Servings: 4

This is the kind of luncheon or supper dish that is just perfect on a hot summer day.

1 envelope unflavored gelatin
2 tbs. tomato juice
1 tsp. lemon juice
½ cup hot chicken stock
¼ cup plain yogurt
2 egg yolks
¼ tsp. curry powder, or to taste

½ jalapeño, seeded, cut into pieces
6 sprigs cilantro
2 cups diced cooked chicken
2 green onions, finely chopped
½ cup finely chopped celery
½ cup finely chopped red bell pepper
1 cup frozen tiny peas, defrosted

Place gelatin, tomato juice, lemon juice and chicken stock in the blender and process until well combined. Add yogurt, egg yolks, curry powder, jalapeño, cilantro and chicken; blend to mix well. Stop and scrape down as necessary. Transfer mixture to a bowl and stir in green onions, celery, red pepper and uncooked peas. Pour into a lightly oiled 4-cup mold and chill until set. Unmold on a platter on a bed of lettuce.

CHILLED TURKEY LOAF

Servings: 4

This tasty dish is an interesting (and yet another) way to use leftover turkey or chicken.

2 cups cooked turkey, no skin or bones
1 envelope unflavored gelatin
½ cup boiling water
juice of ½ lemon
⅔ cup mango chutney
2 green onions, cut into pieces
2 stalks celery, finely chopped
½ green bell pepper, finely chopped
1 cup chicken stock
salt and pepper

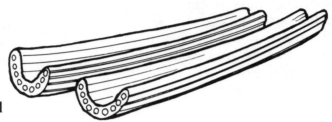

Cut turkey into bite-sized pieces and set aside in a bowl. Place gelatin, boiling water, lemon juice, chutney and green onions in the blender and process until almost smooth. Pour over turkey. Add celery, green pepper, chicken stock, and salt and pepper to taste. Mix well. Pour mixture into a lightly oiled loaf pan and chill until set. Unmold to serve and cut into thick slices.

TUNA-PASTA CASSEROLE

Servings: 4

This is an old standby that goes together quickly with ingredients that are almost always on the pantry shelf.

1½ cups hot milk
1 onion, cut into pieces
6 sprigs parsley
¼ cup flour
4 tbs. butter, room temperature
¼ tsp. oregano
½ tsp. dry mustard

½ tsp. paprika
1 can (6½ oz.) water-packed tuna
3 cups cooked small shell pasta
salt and pepper
½ cup bread crumbs
½ cup grated cheddar cheese

Place milk, onion, parsley, flour, butter, oregano, mustard and paprika in the blender and process until smooth. Flake tuna into a bowl. Add cooked pasta, contents of blender, and salt and pepper to taste. Mix well. Spoon into a 1½-quart buttered casserole. Make bread crumbs in the blender (see page 7) and mix them with grated cheese. Sprinkle bread crumb mixture over top of casserole and bake at 350° for 30 minutes.

NAN'S SALMON MOUSSE

Servings: 8

My good friend (and good cook), Nan, serves this easy and delicious salmon mousse with sliced ripe tomatoes and steamed asparagus for a perfect springtime light meal.

1 envelope plus 1 tsp. unflavored
  gelatin
2 tbs. lemon juice
1 tsp. fresh dill weed or ½ tsp. dried
¼ tsp. paprika
¼ tsp. salt
½ cup boiling water

½ cup mayonnaise
1 small onion, cut into pieces
1 stalk celery, cut into pieces
1 can (16 oz.) salmon, undrained,
  broken up
2 tbs. chopped pimiento
½ cup sour cream

Place gelatin, lemon juice, dill, paprika and salt in the blender. Add boiling water; blend to combine and dissolve gelatin. Add remaining ingredients to blender (in batches, if necessary) and blend to combine. It need not be a fine puree, but should be evenly blended. Pour mixture into a lightly oiled 4-cup mold and chill until set. Unmold to serve.

FISH CUSTARDS

Servings: 4

Make these easy fish custards with drained canned salmon or water-packed tuna or with flaked leftover cooked fish. Serve as a light entrée for lunch or supper.

¾ cup milk
1 cup cooked fish
3 eggs
2 tbs. minced green bell pepper
2 green onions, chopped
3 slices firm white bread, torn into pieces
1 tsp. lemon juice
salt and pepper

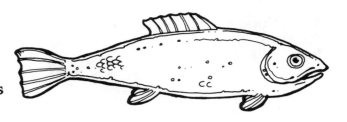

Place all ingredients, except salt and pepper, in the blender and process until well mixed. Add salt and pepper to taste. Spoon mixture into 4 buttered ramekins or custard cups and set in a pan of hot water. Bake at 350° for 30 minutes or until set.

CRAB MOUSSE

Servings: 8

This light and delightful dish is a perfect luncheon or supper entrée. If you do not have a steamer and rack, it's easy to improvise. Choose a pot that is large enough to hold your mold. Loosely crumple several sheets of foil and place them in the bottom of the pot. Press gently to flatten slightly and set the mold on top. Fill the pot almost to the level of the mold with boiling water.

1 lb. skinless, boneless white fish
1 egg
⅛ tsp. cayenne
⅓ cup finely chopped green onions

1 tsp. fresh dill weed or ¼ tsp. dried
1 cup heavy cream
1 lb. fresh crabmeat, picked over
lemon wedges for garnish

Cut fish into small cubes. Place in the blender with egg, cayenne, green onions and dill. Start blending and add cream while the motor is running. Blend until smooth. Add 1 cup crabmeat and continue blending until mixture is smooth again. Transfer to a bowl and fold in remaining crabmeat. Lightly butter a 6-cup ring or other decorative mold and fill with mousse mixture. Smooth top. Set in a steamer on a rack or in a pot on crumpled foil and add boiling water to level of the mold. Cover tightly and steam for 15 minutes or until set. Remove to a rack to cool for 5 minutes. Unmold on a serving dish and wipe away any liquid that accumulates. Serve garnished with lemon wedges.

FRESH CORN PUDDING

Servings: 6

This is a wonderful summer vegetable dish which goes beautifully with grilled poultry and meats.

4 ears corn
2 tsp. sugar
freshly grated nutmeg
salt and pepper
3 eggs
2 cups milk
2 tbs. butter, melted

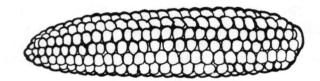

Cut kernels from corn cobs with a sharp knife. Puree corn in the blender with sugar, nutmeg, salt and pepper to taste and eggs. With motor running, add milk and melted butter. Transfer mixture to a buttered 1-quart casserole and place it in a pan of hot water. Bake at 325° for 1 hour or until pudding is set. Serve hot or at room temperature.

MEXICAN ZUCCHINI PUDDING

Servings: 6

Zucchini lovers are always on the look-out for new ways to prepare this year-round vegetable. This pudding is an excellent and unusual choice.

1 cup crushed soda crackers
4 cups sliced zucchini
2 tbs. chopped onion
1 cup grated cheddar cheese
2 eggs
4 tbs. melted butter
nutmeg
salt and pepper

Crush crackers in the blender. Transfer them to a bowl and set aside. Cook zucchini and onion until tender. Drain well and place in blender. Add ⅔ cup cheese, eggs, cracker crumbs, melted butter and seasonings to taste. Blend until well mixed. Transfer mixture to a buttered 1-quart casserole. Top with remaining cheese and bake at 350° for 20 to 25 minutes or until pudding is set.

SCRAMBLED EGGS WITH GOAT CHEESE

Servings: 4

Something special in the scrambled egg department. If you do not care for goat cheese, substitute cream cheese for the same creamy goodness.

8 eggs
⅔ cup half and half
pinch of salt and pepper
4 oz. mild, creamy goat cheese, room temperature, cut into pieces
3 tbs. butter

Place all ingredients except butter in the blender and process until smooth. Heat butter in a nonstick skillet. When it is hot but not brown, pour in egg-cheese mixture. Cook over low heat, stirring with a wooden spoon, until eggs are thick and creamy.

EGGPLANT KUKU

This Persian dish is very much like a soufflé. It is traditionally served with plain yogurt.

4 medium eggplants
6 eggs, separated
¼ cup freshly grated Parmesan cheese
2 cloves garlic, cut into pieces
3 tbs. lemon juice
salt and pepper
2 tbs. butter

Place eggplants on a baking sheet and bake at 350° for about 30 minutes or until very soft. When cool enough to handle, scoop out flesh. In small batches, combine eggplant flesh, egg yolks, Parmesan cheese, garlic and lemon juice in the blender. Blend until smooth. Transfer to a large bowl and add salt and pepper to taste. Beat egg whites to soft peaks and fold into eggplant mixture. Melt butter in a deep 9-inch baking dish and pour in eggplant. Bake at 350° for 30 minutes or until puffed and brown. Serve immediately with plain yogurt.

ENTRÈES AND SIDE DISHES   115

A QUARTET OF VEGETABLE PUREES

Servings: 4

This is more complicated than simply cooking up the veggies, but the result is both beautiful and delicious and worth the trouble every now and then.

1¼ lb. ripe tomatoes, peeled, seeded, coarsely chopped
1 clove garlic, cut into pieces
salt and pepper
1¼ lb. red bell peppers, stemmed, seeded, coarsely chopped
1 lb. fennel, trimmed, cut into pieces
1 lb. green beans, trimmed
1-1½ cups heavy cream

Combine tomatoes and garlic in a nonstick skillet. Season with salt and pepper and cook over medium heat, stirring occasionally, until almost dry. Spoon into the blender and puree. Season with salt and pepper and set aside.

In a small pan, combine peppers with 2 tbs. water and cook over medium heat until very tender. Stir occasionally. Puree in blender and strain to remove skins. Season with salt and pepper and set aside.

Cook fennel in boiling, salted water until very tender. Drain and puree in blender. Strain, season with salt and pepper and set aside.

Cook green beans in boiling salted water until very tender. Drain and puree in blender. Strain, season with salt and pepper and set aside. The vegetables can be prepared to this point several hours ahead.

To serve: Reheat all the purees (separately) over medium heat. Stir in just enough cream to bring each to a thick soup consistency. Spoon equal amounts of each puree into each of 4 large flat soup plates. Tap plates lightly on a flat surface and then swirl decoratively with a spoon. Serve hot as a separate course.

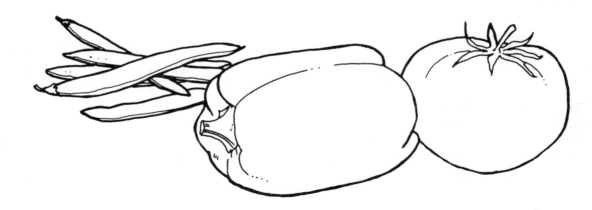

CARROT-RASPBERRY PUREE

Servings: 6

This is an unusual and exceptionally good combination.

1¼ lb. carrots, peeled, sliced
3 tbs. butter
salt
¾ cup frozen raspberries
1 tbs. raspberry vinegar
1 tbs. creme de cassis
sugar to taste

Place carrots and 2 tbs. butter in a saucepan with a small amount of water and cook until carrots are very tender. Drain and reserve liquid. Puree carrots in the blender, adding just enough reserved liquid to make a smooth puree. Transfer puree to the top of a double boiler and keep warm over hot water. Add salt to taste. Defrost raspberries in a strainer, reserving juice. Combine vinegar, cassis, sugar and ½ tbs. reserved juice in a saucepan and reduce by half over high heat. Add remaining tablespoon of butter and raspberries and remove from heat immediately. Gently swirl raspberry mixture into warm carrots and serve at once.

CELERY ROOT PUREE

Servings: 4-6

Celery root is also called celeric. It tastes like stalks of celery but it is adaptable to different uses. Peel it with a vegetable peeler.

2 medium onions, sliced
1 tbs. olive or canola oil
4 celery roots, peeled, cubed
1 bay leaf
4-6 cups chicken stock
half and half
salt and pepper

Sauté onions in oil until soft. Add celery roots, bay leaf and chicken stock to cover and simmer until celery root is very tender, 30 to 45 minutes. Remove bay leaf and puree mixture in small batches in blender. Add half and half to desired consistency and season with salt and pepper.

CARROTS SUPREME

An easy way to prepare carrots. Let them simmer in the oven while the rest of the meal cooks.

2 cups carrots, peeled, thinly sliced
½ cup water
2 tbs. parsley leaves
½ tsp. salt
4 tbs. soft butter

Place carrots, water, parsley and salt in the blender and process until almost smooth. Transfer to a small ovenproof dish or casserole and stir in butter. Cover tightly (use foil if your dish has no cover) and bake at 325° for 30 minutes.

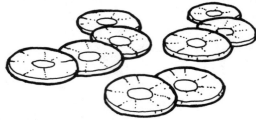

DESSERTS

WALNUT MEAL CAKE

Put the layers together with jam or marmalade and dust the top with confectioners' sugar. This light-as-a-feather cake couldn't be easier.

2 tbs. flour
2½ tsp. baking powder
4 eggs
¾ cup sugar
1 cup walnuts

Butter two 8-inch layer cake pans. Combine flour and baking powder and set aside. In the blender, combine eggs and sugar until mixture is smooth and light. With motor running, add nuts, one at a time, and blend until finely ground. Add flour mixture all at once and blend until it is just combined. Divide batter between 2 pans and bake at 350° for 20 minutes or until cakes test done. Invert pans on a rack to cool before removing cakes from pans.

BUTTERMILK POPPY SEED CAKE

Yield: 1 bundt cake

Poppy seeds are especially popular in the baked goods of Central Europe where they are almost always ground first in special poppy seed grinders. The blender works beautifully for this task, which greatly improves the flavor. Soaking the ground seeds further enhances their flavor. Soak them in the liquid called for in the recipe and add both at the same time. Grind the seeds in the blender, about ¼ cup at a time.

⅓ cup poppy seeds
1 cup buttermilk
1 cup butter or margarine, softened
1½ cups sugar
3 eggs
½ tsp. vanilla

2¼ cups flour
3 tsp. baking powder
1 tsp. cinnamon
½ tsp. salt
1½ tsp. grated lemon peel
confectioners' sugar

Grind poppy seeds in the blender. Combine with buttermilk and set aside. Cream butter and sugar until light and fluffy. Beat in eggs and vanilla and combine well. Combine flour, baking powder, cinnamon and salt. Add dry ingredients to creamed mixture alternately with buttermilk. Stir in lemon peel. Pour batter into a buttered 9-cup bundt pan and bake at 350° for 50 minutes or until cake tests done. Cool for 10 minutes; remove from pan to cool completely on a rack. Dust top with confectioners' sugar.

ORANGE-ALMOND CAKE

This dense, moist cake has its origins in the Middle East. It's a slow baker but well worth the wait.

2 large seedless navel oranges
6 eggs
1½ cups ground almonds
pinch of salt
1 cup sugar
1 tsp. baking powder

Wash oranges and boil in water to cover, without peeling, until very soft, about 30 minutes. Remove oranges from water and cool. Cut oranges into quarters and remove any seeds. In batches, process oranges in the blender to a medium-fine puree. Beat eggs in a bowl until thick. Add ground almonds (which may also be done in the blender), salt, sugar, baking powder and ground oranges. Mix well. Pour batter into a buttered, floured, deep 9-inch cake pan or springform pan. Bake at 400° for 1 hour or longer, until cake is firm to the touch. Cool on a rack. Serve with whipped cream, if desired.

ALMOND TORTE

Servings: 10

Grinding the almonds with the flour keeps them from becoming oily. This is a wonderful cake for a company dessert.

2 cups blanched almonds
1 tbs. flour
6 eggs, separated
1 tsp. cream of tartar
1¾ cups sugar
½ tsp. vanilla

1 cup water
1 cinnamon stick
1 tbs. grated orange peel
1 tsp. orange flavored liqueur
¼ cup toasted chopped almonds

Preheat oven to 325°. Butter and flour a 9-inch springform pan. In the blender, combine blanched almonds and flour to a fine meal. Set aside. In a large bowl, beat egg whites until they are frothy. Add cream of tartar and continue to beat, adding 1 cup of sugar gradually. When stiff peaks are formed, beat in egg yolks, one at a time, and then vanilla. Fold in almond flour and transfer batter to prepared pan. Bake 25 to 25 minutes. Cool 5 minutes. Turn out of pan onto a deep plate. Heat water with ¾ cup sugar, cinnamon stick and orange peel. Simmer 5 minutes. Remove from heat and remove cinnamon stick. Stir in liqueur and pour syrup over torte. Sprinkle with chopped almonds. Cool before serving.

OLD WORLD TORTE

Here's another fine party dessert with the illusive flavor of poppy seeds. All the ingredients should be at room temperature before starting.

1 cup poppy seeds
1/3 cup flour
1/3 cup cornstarch
1 tsp. baking powder
10 tbs. butter
2/3 cup sugar

4 eggs, separated
1 tsp. sherry
1 tsp. vanilla
1 tsp. finely grated lemon peel
1/4 cup milk

In the blender, in 3 batches, grind poppy seeds until fine. Set aside. Combine flour, cornstarch and baking powder and set aside. Cream butter and 1/3 cup sugar until fluffy. Add egg yolks, one at a time. Stir in sherry, vanilla, lemon peel and poppy seeds. Stir in flour mixture alternately with milk. Beat egg whites to soft peaks. Gradually add 1/3 cup sugar and continue beating until fluffy. Fold whites evenly into batter and pour into prepared pan. Bake 45 minutes or until center tests done. Cool 15 minutes and then remove from pan. Serve with whipped cream and/or fruit, if desired.

APRICOT-WALNUT TORTE

This richly flavored cake belies its great simplicity.

½ lb. dried apricots
½ cup water
¼ lb. shelled walnuts
¾ cup sugar
6 eggs, separated

Preheat oven to 325°. Butter and flour a 9-inch cake pan. Simmer apricots in water until soft. Drain and place in the blender. Add nuts and sugar and process to a fairly smooth puree. Transfer to a bowl, add egg yolks and mix well. Beat egg whites to form soft peaks and fold into apricot mixture. Turn batter into prepared pan and bake for 1 hour or until cake tests done. Cool in pan.

CRUMB CRUSTS

It takes less than a minute to make a crumb crust with the blender to help you.

GRAHAM CRACKER CRUMB CRUST

Yield: one 8-9-inch pie crust

12-14 whole graham crackers, broken
  into pieces
¼ cup sugar

½ tsp. cinnamon, optional
8 tbs. melted butter

Combine crackers, sugar and cinnamon in the blender and blend to a smooth meal. Transfer mixture to a bowl and stir in melted butter. Empty mixture into an 8- or 9-inch pie plate and press evenly over bottom and up sides. Chill 1 hour before filling.

GINGERSNAP CRUMB CRUST

Yield: one 8-9-inch pie crust

32 gingersnaps
3 tbs. confectioners' sugar

4 tbs. melted butter

With motor running, add gingersnaps to the blender one at a time. Transfer crumbs to a bowl and stir in sugar. Stir in melted butter. Pour onto an 8- or 9-inch pie plate and press evenly over bottom and up sides. Bake at 400° for 8 minutes. Cool.

THANKSGIVING CHEESECAKE

Servings: 16

Serve this All-American cheesecake in small portions. It's as rich as it is delicious.

1 crumb crust of choice, page 129
2 lb. cream cheese, softened, in pieces
1 cup sugar

4 eggs
1 cup sour cream
grated peel of 1 orange

Prepare crust. Place 1 lb. cream cheese, 1/2 cup sugar, 2 eggs and 1/2 cup sour cream in the blender and process until very smooth. Transfer to a bowl and repeat with remaining cheese, sugar, eggs and sour cream. Stir in orange peel. Pour batter into crust and bake at 325° for 45 minutes. Turn off heat and let cheesecake cool completely in the oven. When cool, transfer to the refrigerator and chill overnight.

TOPPING

2 cups cranberries, fresh or frozen
1 cup sugar
1/2 cup water

2 tsp. cornstarch
2 tbs. water
grated peel of 1 orange

Combine cranberries, sugar and 1/2 cup water in a saucepan. Cover and cook until cranberries begin to pop. Mix cornstarch with 2 tbs. water and stir into cranberries. Cook 2 or 3 minutes or until slightly thickened. Stir in orange peel. Cool. Chill thoroughly. Spread on cheesecake just before serving.

BITE-SIZED CHEESECAKES

Maybe these really are two-bite sized, at least in polite company. They are delicious and perfect additions to a plate of tiny desserts.

12 vanilla wafers
2 pkg. (8 oz. each) cream cheese, room temperature, cut into pieces
2 eggs
½ cup sugar
1 tsp. vanilla

Line mini muffin tins with foil liners. Place 1 vanilla wafer in the bottom of each liner. In the blender, combine remaining ingredients and process until smooth. Spoon batter over wafers, filling each ¾ full. Bake at 325° for 25 minutes. Cool in pan; chill in the refrigerator. Top with fresh berries or fruit at serving time.

SWEDISH APPLESAUCE CAKE

This dessert is very simple, very good and not too sweet.

1 box zwieback, broken into pieces
2 cups applesauce
6 tbs. butter

Add zwieback to the blender with motor running. Blend to fine crumbs. Melt butter in a skillet and add crumbs. Stir to brown evenly, being careful not to burn. Butter an 8-or 9-inch pie plate and arrange applesauce and crumbs in alternate layers ending with crumbs. Bake at 375° for 30 minutes. Cool and serve with sweetened whipped cream, if desired.

CHERRY CLAFOUTI

Servings: 2

A clafouti is a French fruit pudding something akin to our cobbler. It can be made with any fresh seasonal fruit and is especially delicious with cherries or with plump, juicy blackberries. This recipe is easily doubled or tripled, but do it in small batches in the blender.

⅓ cup plus 1 tbs. sugar
2 tbs. flour
2 eggs
⅔ cup milk
1½ tsp. vanilla
¼ tsp. salt
1 cup cherries, pitted, cut in half
½ tbs. butter, cut into pieces

Preheat oven to 400°. Place ⅓ cup sugar, flour, eggs, milk, vanilla and salt in the blender and process just until smooth. In one 3-cup or two individual buttered gratin dishes, place a single layer of cherries. Pour custard mixture over and bake for 20 to 25 minutes or until top is puffed. Sprinkle remaining sugar on top and dot with butter. Return to oven to melt butter. Serve warm with ice cream, if desired.

BASIC BUTTER CREAM FROSTING

Yield: 1½ cups

This is a simple, no-fail basic recipe.

3 tbs. hot cream or milk
4 tbs. butter, room temperature, cut into pieces
1 tsp. vanilla
2½ cups confectioners' sugar

Blend cream, butter and vanilla until smooth. With motor running, gradually add sugar and blend until smooth.

VARIATIONS

- **Orange or Lemon Butter Cream Frosting:** Substitute ¼ cup frozen orange juice concentrate or ¼ cup lemon juice for the cream and vanilla in the basic recipe.

- **Coffee Butter Cream Frosting:** Substitute 2 tbs. instant coffee powder for the vanilla in the basic recipe.

- **Butterscotch Butter Cream Frosting:** Substitute 1 cup brown sugar for 1 cup of confectioners' sugar in the basic recipe.

BEST EVER CHOCOLATE
BUTTER CREAM FROSTING

Yield: 1 cup

This recipe is one of the best and makes enough frosting for the tops of two 8-inch layers.

1 pkg. (6 oz.) chocolate bits
¼ cup boiling water or strong coffee
2 tbs. confectioners' sugar
4 egg yolks
½ cup butter, cut into pieces
2 tbs. rum or other liquid

Place chocolate bits in the blender and process briefly. Scrape down sides, add hot liquid and blend again, briefly. Add sugar, egg yolks, butter and rum. Blend until smooth.

NOTE: In hot weather, the frosting may need refrigeration to reach spreading consistency.

CHOCOLATE POTS DE CREME

Servings: 6

Very rich, very delicious. When it's time for a special treat, this quickly-made dessert is hard to beat. For a mocha flavor, add 2 tbs. instant coffee to the milk.

¾ cup milk
1 cup chocolate bits
1 egg
2 tbs. sugar
1 tsp. vanilla
pinch of salt

Heat milk just to a boil. Place all other ingredients in the blender. Add hot milk and blend for 1 minute. Pour into 6 pots de creme or other small serving dishes. Chill for several hours.

BAKED RICOTTA PUDDING

Servings: 8

This simple dessert comes with its own built-in sauce on the bottom. Serve it with fresh berries or other fruit, if desired.

2 cups ricotta cheese
1 cup half and half
3 eggs, separated
½ cup sugar
¼ tsp. almond extract
½ tsp. grated lemon peel

In the blender, combine ricotta cheese, half and half, egg yolks, 6 tbs. sugar and almond extract. Blend until smooth. Stir in lemon peel. In a small bowl, beat egg whites until foamy. Gradually add 2 tbs. sugar, beating to soft peaks. Fold in cheese mixture and pour batter into a buttered 1½- or 2-quart casserole. Set casserole in a pan of hot water and bake at 350° for 30 minutes or until center is set and firm to the touch. Serve warm or cool.

COEUR A LA CREME

You will need the special heart-shaped, porcelain draining dish in which this lovely French dessert is traditionally made. They are available, in both large and individual sizes, at specialty cookware stores.

1 lb. cottage cheese
½ cup heavy cream
1 lb. cream cheese, room temperature, cut into pieces
1 tsp. salt
½ tsp. lemon extract
½ cup sugar

In several batches, place cottage cheese and heavy cream in the blender and process until it is completely smooth. With motor running, add remaining ingredients and continue to blend until mixture is very smooth. Pour batter into a heart-shaped porcelain draining mold lined with damp cheesecloth. Set on a plate to drain in the refrigerator overnight. To serve, invert the mold on a serving platter and carefully remove cheesecloth. Serve with fresh berries or *Raspberry Sauce*, page 64.

APRICOT CUSTARD PIE

This versatile dessert is delicious, low cal and easy to prepare. It may be made as a custard instead of a pie.

1 can (16 oz.) apricots, drained, pitted
½ cup milk
⅓ cup sugar
1 tsp. vanilla
¼ tsp. salt
¼ tsp. ground ginger
1 cup milk
4 eggs
one 9-inch pie shell, partially baked

Place apricots, ½ cup milk, sugar, vanilla, salt and ginger in the blender and puree until smooth. Remove to a bowl. Beat together 1 cup milk and eggs and pour mixture through a strainer into apricot mixture. Pour into a partially baked pie shell or into a 1-quart ovenproof dish and bake at 350° for 45 to 60 minutes or until custard is set. Cool and refrigerate for several hours.

PAPAYA CUSTARD PIE

Servings: 6-8

For most of us, papayas are a special treat. This smooth tropical custard pie is an extra special treat.

1 large ripe papaya
3 eggs
⅔ cup sugar
1 cup half and half
1 tsp. vanilla
one 9-inch pie shell, partially baked

Cut papaya in half. Scrape out and discard seeds; peel. Cut ¼ into thin slices and reserve. Cut remaining fruit into chunks and puree in the blender with eggs, sugar, half and half and vanilla. Pour mixture into pie shell and bake at 425° for 15 minutes. Reduce heat to 350° and continue to bake until custard is set, about 15 to 20 minutes. Let cool 30 minutes and serve warm topped with reserved papaya slices.

MAGIC PUMPKIN PIE

This is about the easiest pumpkin pie imaginable and it's always perfect.

one 9-inch pie shell, baked at 375° for 10 minutes
2 cups cooked pumpkin (canned OK)
1 can sweetened condensed milk (not evaporated milk)
1 egg
½ tsp. salt
½ tsp. ground ginger
¾ tsp. cinnamon

Combine all ingredients in the blender and process until smooth. It may be necessary to do this in 2 batches. Pour mixture into prepared pie shell and bake at 375° for about 50 minutes, or until a knife inserted in the center comes out clean. Cool and refrigerate at least 1 hour. Serve with whipped cream, if desired.

APRICOT CHIFFON PIE

Yield: one 8-or 9-inch pie

*This creamy pie is delicious with a **Gingersnap Crumb Crust**, or you may make it with a **Graham Cracker Crumb Crust**, both on page 129.*

1½ tsp. unflavored gelatin
1 tbs. lime juice
¾ cup dried apricots
1 cup water
½ cup plus 3 tbs. sugar
½ cup apple juice
½ cup sour cream or plain yogurt
3 egg whites, room temperature
1 crumb crust, page 129

Soften gelatin in lime juice for 5 minutes. Combine apricots, water and ½ cup sugar in a saucepan and simmer for 20 minutes. Transfer to the blender and puree until smooth. Add lime juice and softened gelatin and combine thoroughly. Add apple juice and combine again. Transfer to a bowl and cool. Fold in sour cream. Beat egg whites with 3 tbs. sugar to soft peaks and fold into apricot mixture. Turn into prepared shell. Chill at least 6 hours.

MANGO CUSTARD

Servings: 6-8

The combination of mangos, limes and rum is almost enough to transport you to the Caribbean.

2 ripe mangos, peeled, seeded
½ cup sugar, or to taste
2 tbs. rum
3 tbs. fresh lime juice
3 eggs
½ cup heavy cream

Cut mangos into small pieces and puree in the blender with sugar, rum and lime juice. With motor running, add eggs. Transfer mixture to the top of a double boiler over boiling water. Cook and stir until mixture becomes custard-like. Pour into a serving bowl or into individual dishes and refrigerate several hours. At serving time, garnish with whipped cream.

MELON CUSTARD

A custard with a different flair.

1 cantaloupe
honey to taste
2 cups half and half
8 eggs

Cut cantaloupe in half and discard seeds. Peel ½ and cut flesh into small pieces. Puree pieces in the blender, adding more if necessary to make 1 cup puree. Sweeten to taste with honey. Bring half and half just to a boil in a saucepan. Remove from heat and stir in melon puree. Beat eggs and pour them through a strainer into custard. Pour into 6 individual ramekins or other ovenproof dishes. Place dishes in a pan of hot water and bake at 300° for 20 to 30 minutes or until custard is set. Cool and refrigerate for several hours. Garnish custards at serving time with melon balls cut from remaining melon.

APRICOT MOUSSE

This French-inspired mousse is made from dried apricots so it can be enjoyed year round.

1 lemon
1 lb. dried apricots, soaked in water, drained
1 cup applesauce
½ cup sugar, or to taste
4 egg whites
toasted, slivered almonds for garnish

With a vegetable peeler, peel yellow part of peel from lemon. Juice lemon. In a saucepan, simmer lemon peel, juice, apricots and applesauce for 30 minutes. Drain any excess juice and puree mixture in the blender. Cool and add sugar to taste. Beat egg whites to soft peaks and fold into apricot mixture. Spoon mousse into a serving dish and chill for several hours. Garnish with almonds before serving, if desired.

MANGO MOUSSE

This delicious dessert can be prepared either of two ways — lean or lavish. Whatever your choice, the mangos must be fully ripe, juicy and fragrant.

5 lbs. ripe mangos, peeled, pitted, coarsely chopped
½ cup fresh lime juice
½ cup sugar
1 envelope unflavored gelatin
¼ cup water
2 egg whites, room temperature
½ cup heavy cream, well chilled

In the blender, puree mangos with lime juice and sugar. Do it in several batches, if necessary. Sprinkle gelatin over water in a saucepan and let stand for 10 minutes; stir over low heat to dissolve. Allow to cool slightly and add to mango puree. Beat egg whites to soft peaks. Beat cream to soft peaks and combine gently with egg whites. Fold into mango mixture. Pour into a serving bowl or individual dishes and chill for several hours. For the lean version: use 4 egg whites and omit the heavy cream.

STRAWBERRY MOUSSE

Servings: 8

This taste-of-springtime recipe is a native of Austria and makes a beautiful party dessert.

1½ quarts strawberries, washed, stemmed
½ cup sugar
½ cup white wine
2 envelopes unflavored gelatin
½ cup cold water
½ cup boiling water
2 cups heavy cream, whipped

In batches, combine strawberries, sugar and wine in blender and process until smooth. Transfer to a bowl and chill. Soften gelatin in cold water. Add boiling water and stir to dissolve. Cool and combine with chilled strawberry mixture. Beat with a rotary beater until fluffy and slightly thickened. Fold in whipped cream. Turn mixture into a lightly oiled 2-quart mold or into 8 individual dishes. Chill for at least 3 hours. If using a mold, unmold on a platter to serve.

TIPS FOR MAKING FROZEN DESSERTS

- Frozen desserts tend to form crystals after long freezer storage. To make them smooth again, allow them to soften slightly and then remix in the blender. Refreeze for several hours before serving.

- Make the simple syrup (equal parts sugar and water) ahead of time and keep it in the refrigerator. It will be ready to add to pureed fruit for a quick fruit puree ice.

- Always adjust the sweetness in any recipe to suit your taste, but remember that freezing decreases the intensity of sugar and honey.

- Always taste before you freeze. Sometimes the addition of a squeeze of lemon juice adds just the right counterpoint to an otherwise bland fruit puree.

- Super fine sugar is best for water ices because it dissolves easily. It is easily made by whirring regular granulated sugar in the blender.

- A general rule about proportions calls for 2 cups fruit, 1-1½ cups liquid and ½ cup sugar. Extra ripe, seasonal fruit will add to the liquid and will probably also require less sugar.

BASIC FRUIT SORBET

Servings: 4-6

This basic fruit sorbet is about as uncomplicated as it gets, but the finished product is packed with intense fruit flavor.

2 cups fresh or frozen fruit
2 tbs. simple syrup

2 tbs. lemon or lime juice, or to taste

Puree pieces of fruit to a smooth puree in the blender. Strain, if desired. Combine puree with remaining ingredients. Pour into a shallow bowl or pan and freeze until slushy. Spoon into the blender and blend until smooth. Return to freezer until firm.

PERSIMMON SORBET

Servings: 4-6

Persimmons are a wonderful fall fruit. Make persimmon puree by whirring ripe, unpeeled persimmons in the blender until smooth.

2 cups persimmon puree, about 4
  persimmons
1 cup water

3 tbs. lime or lemon juice
1 tsp. grated lime or lemon peel
½ cup sugar

Combine all ingredients in the blender and mix. Pour into a shallow bowl or pan and freeze until slushy. Remix in blender and return to freezer until firm.

JOYCE'S PINEAPPLE SORBET

Servings: 6

This simple dessert takes full advantage of a juicy, fragrant pineapple.

1 medium fresh, ripe pineapple
3/4 cup sugar

2 1/2 tbs. lemon juice

Peel and core pineapple and cut it into chunks. In small batches, puree all ingredients together in the blender. Pour into a shallow bowl or pan and freeze until slushy. Remix in blender and return to freezer until firm.

GRAPEFRUIT SORBET

Servings: 4

This is also good made with oranges instead of grapefruit, or try a combination of the two. Adjust the sugar, if necessary.

2 cups water
1 cup sugar

1 cup fresh grapefruit juice
zest of 1 grapefruit

Heat water and sugar until sugar dissolves. Add juice and zest and pour into a shallow bowl or pan. Cool. Freeze until slushy. Spoon into blender and puree until smooth. Return to freezer until firm.

MELON SORBET WITH GINGER

Yield: 1 quart

Melons and ginger are a wonderful flavor combination. Any ripe melon makes this a delightfully refreshing dessert for a hot day.

⅔ cup sugar
⅔ cup water
½ large melon, enough to make 3 cups puree
½ cup orange juice
2 tbs. lime juice
3 tbs. minced candied ginger
1 tsp. grated lime peel
1 egg white

Combine sugar and water in a saucepan and heat until sugar is dissolved. Cool. Puree melon in the blender and measure 3 cups. Add syrup, orange juice, lime juice, ginger and lime peel; blend until smooth. Pour into a shallow pan or bowl and freeze until slushy. Return to blender. Add egg white and blend until smooth. Return to freezer until firm.

MAUI PAPAYA SHERBET

Servings: 6

Undeniably, a taste of the Islands. Papaya and orange are a terrific combination.

½ cup orange juice
¼ cup lemon juice
1 papaya, peeled, seeded, diced

1 cup sugar
2 cups half and half

Place orange and lime juices and papaya in the blender and process until smooth. Pour into a bowl and add sugar and half and half. Stir until sugar is dissolved. Pour into a shallow bowl or pan and freeze until slushy. Return to blender and remix. Freeze until firm.

FRESH PEACH ICE CREAM

Yield: 1 quart

This is rich and smooth and heady with the flavor of summer.

4 peaches
1 cup heavy cream
¼ cup sugar

juice of ½ lime
peach or raspberry liqueur, optional

Peel and pit peaches. Cut into pieces and puree in blender. Add remaining ingredients and process until smooth. Freeze in an electric or hand turned ice cream maker.

JAM ICE CREAM

Yield: about 1 quart

This ice cream is so easy to make and works well with just about any jam, preserve or marmalade.

1 cup jam, preserves or marmalade
2 cups half and half

½ tsp. vanilla
pinch of salt

Combine all ingredients in the blender and process until smooth. Pour into an electric or hand turned ice cream freezer and freeze according to the manufacturer's instructions.

BANANA ICE CREAM

Yield: about 1 quart

For an added flavor boost, add ½ cup raisins after removing from the blender.

4 ripe bananas, cut into pieces
juice of ½ lemon
1 cup sugar

2¼ cups half and half
2-3 tbs. dark rum, optional

Combine bananas and lemon juice in the blender in two batches. Add remaining ingredients and blend until smooth. Freeze in an electric or hand turned ice cream freezer.

BEVERAGES OF ALL KINDS

Blender health drinks, often called smoothies, have come into their own in recent years. In addition to tasting good, they are an easy way to get your nutrients on the run. I've even heard that some people assemble all the ingredients for their morning energizer in the blender container the night before and place it in the refrigerator. In the morning — set the container on the blender, a few short spins and breakfast is ready.

In Latin America, blender fruit and milk drinks called *batidas* and *vitaminas* are part of the culture. Of course, they take advantage of luscious, tree-ripened tropical fruits. Avocado-milk drinks are also popular, both sweet and savory. In many cases, coconut milk, or coconut milk in combination with cow's milk, make the Latin American drinks both smooth and rich.

Combinations are almost endless. Often-used ingredients include milk, buttermilk, yogurt, cottage cheese, eggs, honey, sherbet, ice cream, mixed fruit juices, vegetable juices, fruits, wheat germ, protein powder and even peanut butter.

Some people keep a container of mixed fruit or mixed fruit juices on hand in the refrigerator. The addition of bananas, which should not be refrigerated, make the drinks especially smooth.

Protein powder, available at health food stores, is a healthy addition but imparts a slightly chalky taste.

If fresh fruit juice is not available, a spoonful or two of frozen juice concentrate adds both substance and an intense flavor boost. If using frozen fruits or berries, do not thaw first. Use the following recipes as they are or to spark your imagination.

Alcoholic blender drinks are also included in this chapter. The blender is a wonderfully valuable aid to home entertaining or for other occasions when "an adult beverage" is desired.

BREAKFAST SMOOTHIE

Servings: 1

Everything you need for a complete breakfast. Just blend and enjoy.

⅔ cup orange juice
⅔ cup mixed fruit juice
1 egg

1 banana, cut into pieces
1 tsp. wheat germ

Combine all ingredients in the blender until smooth.

BANANA SMOOTHIE

Servings: 1

This is a classic smoothie. Use it as a basic recipe and vary it to suit your taste, or what you have on hand. The banana, in addition to being very nutritious, gives the drink body and makes it really smooth.

1 ripe banana, cut into pieces
1 cup yogurt, plain or flavored

2 tbs. honey, or to taste, if desired
½ tsp. vanilla

Combine all ingredients in the blender until smooth.

PEANUT SMOOTHIE

Servings: 1

This smoothie is great for lunch or a snack.

1 cup milk
1 cup vanilla ice cream

2 tbs. peanut butter
1 tbs. protein powder

Combine all ingredients in the blender until smooth.

ORANGE SMOOTHIE

Servings: 1

If you're looking for a truly simple but delicious recipe, this is it.

2 cups milk

3 tbs. frozen orange juice concentrate

Combine both ingredients in the blender until smooth.

APRICOT SMOOTHIE

Servings: 1

If dried apricots are used, soak them first in warm water. Drain before combining with the other ingredients.

8 apricots
2/3 cup plain yogurt

2/3 cup mixed fruit juice
1 tbs. wheat germ

Combine all ingredients in the blender until smooth.

CUCUMBER SMOOTHIE

Servings: 1

This is the ultimate refreshing lunch on a hot day.

¾ cup milk
¾ cup plain yogurt
½ medium cucumber, peeled, seeded,
  cut into pieces

1 tbs. sliced green onion
pinch of salt
2-3 mint leaves

Combine all ingredients in the blender until smooth.

FROSTIE FRUIT SMOOTHIE

Servings: 1

Crushed ice makes this drink extra cold and refreshing.

½ banana, cut into pieces
¼ cup apple juice
¼ cup cranberry juice
¼ cup white grape juice

¼ cup pineapple juice
¼ cup orange juice
¾ cup crushed ice

Combine all ingredients in the blender until smooth.

TANGERINE-BUTTERMILK SMOOTHIE

Servings: 1

This drink strays slightly from the strictly health food category, but it's tangy and delicious.

2/3 cup tangerine sherbet
2/3 cup buttermilk

2/3 cup mixed fruit juice

Combine all ingredients in the blender until smooth.

MOCHA SMOOTHIE

Servings: 1

If you like mocha, you'll love this.

2 tbs. instant cocoa powder
1 tsp. instant coffee powder
2 tbs. hot water

2 tbs. sugar
2 cups cold milk

Dissolve cocoa and coffee powders in water. Transfer to the blender and add remaining ingredients. Blend until smooth.

NADA COLADA

Cream of coconut is canned under the name Coco Lopez. This is the nonalcoholic version of the popular Pina Colada (see page 162 for the alcoholic version).

1 oz. cream of coconut

1 cup crushed ice

2 oz. unsweetened pineapple juice

Combine all ingredients in the blender until smooth.

BUTTERMILK COOLER

This is a versatile drink. What fruits do you like and what do you have on hand? Supplies of "fruit mixes" ready and waiting in the refrigerator will make this satisfying drink a real quickie.

For each cup of fresh berries or fruit (one fruit or a combination) add:

¼ cup sugar

½ tsp. vanilla

For each single drink blend together until smooth:

¼ cup fruit mixture (above)

1 cup buttermilk

¼ cup crushed ice, optional

BASIC SPARKLING FRUIT COOLER

Servings: 2

It's not easy to imagine anything more refreshing on a hot day or evening than a sparkling fruit cooler. For an elegant touch, chill two long-stemmed balloon wine glasses in the freezer for 5 minutes before filling them with this delicious indulgence.

fruit: strawberries, raspberries, peaches, apricots, papaya, pineapple, mango or
  any combination
lemon juice
sugar
ice cubes
sparkling water
mint or fresh berry for garnish

In the blender, puree peeled, seeded pieces of fruit until smooth. Add lemon juice and sugar to taste. Into a 14-16 oz. glass, spoon ⅔ cup fruit puree. Add ice cubes and fill glass with sparkling water. Stir to blend. Garnish with mint or a whole fresh berry or two and serve at once.

JUAN'S KILLER MARGARITAS

Servings: 2

This recipe comes to me from a true aficionado who stresses the importance of high quality tequila and freshly squeezed lime juice.

2 oz. gold tequila
2 oz. Triple Sec

juice of 6-8 limes
10 ice cubes, slightly crushed

Combine all ingredients in the blender and blend at high speed until frothy. Pour and enjoy.

PINA COLADA

Servings: 1

This popular drink has joined those which are considered "classics."

1 oz. cream of coconut
2 oz. unsweetened pineapple juice

1½ oz. light rum
5-6 ice cubes, slightly crushed (1 cup)

Combine all ingredients in the blender and process until smooth. Serve at once.

STRAWBERRY MARGARITAS

On a hot summer evening, what's more delectable than a Strawberry Margarita? Possibly a Strawberry Daiquiri.

1½ pints strawberries, stems removed   juice of 1 lime
5-6 ice cubes, slightly crushed (l cup)   1½ oz. gold tequila

Combine all ingredients in the blender and blend at low speed until smooth. Serve at once.

STRAWBERRY DAIQUIRI

Servings: 2

Calling all daiquiri lovers. This recipe serves two in great style.

½ pint fresh strawberries, stems removed   juice of one lime
5-6 ice cubes, slightly crushed (1 cup)   1½ oz. light rum

Combine all ingredients in the blender and blend at low speed until smooth. Serve at once.

BLOODY MARY SORBET

Servings: 4

If you're looking for something different for your next Sunday brunch, this may be the answer. It may be made with or without vodka but will freeze a little harder without.

1 cup tomato juice
3 oz. vodka, optional
juice of 2 lemons
1 egg white
salt and pepper to taste
dash of cayenne or Tabasco Sauce
dash of Worcestershire sauce
5-6 ice cubes, slightly crushed (1 cup)
cilantro sprigs to garnish

Place all ingredients, except cilantro, in the blender and blend at high speed until smooth. Pour into a shallow pan or bowl and freeze. Just before serving, blend again and pour into long-stemmed glasses. Garnish with cilantro and serve at once.

THE BELLINI A LA HARRY'S BAR

In Venice, Harry's Bar is a watering hole of long standing and, at Harry's Bar, this seductive concoction is the drink of choice. It was invented sometime in the 1950s.

2-3 ripe peaches (to make 1 cup puree)
1 bottle champagne
2 oz. cognac
peach slices for garnish

Pit peaches but do not peel. Cut them up and puree in the blender. Remove puree from blender, measure 1 cup and divide into thirds. Return 1/3 to blender. Add 1/3 of the champagne and 1/3 of the cognac and blend briefly. Take care not to make mixture foamy. Transfer to a bowl and repeat with the other 2/3.

Freeze mixture until crystals form, about 1 hour. Stir to break up crystals and return to freezer for 30 minutes. Stir again and serve in champagne glasses. Garnish each drink with a peach slice.

RASPBERRY SANGRIA

Yield: 6 cups

Pureed raspberries give this refreshing summer drink a delightful flavor boost.

1 quart fresh or frozen (unsweetened)
 raspberries
1 quart dry white wine

sugar to taste
ice cubes
orange and lime slices

If using frozen berries, defrost. Puree berries in the blender. Strain to remove seeds. Combine raspberry puree with wine. Add sugar to taste. Pour over ice cubes in a large pitcher. Serve in tall glasses garnished with orange and lime slices.

RASPBERRY LIQUEUR

Yield: almost 4 cups

Nice to have on hand for sipping, for flavoring and for serving over ice cream.

2 cups 80 proof vodka
⅔ cup sugar

12 oz. bag frozen raspberries, defrosted

In several batches, puree all ingredients in the blender for 30 seconds. Pour into a quart jar. Stir and let stand for 10 minutes to let some air escape. Cover jar tightly and store in a cool place for 4-5 days. Shake gently once or twice. Strain through a coffee filter directly into a glass coffee pot or glass bowl. Do this in 3 batches and do not stir or hurry the process. Store in a beautiful decanter to show off your handiwork.

INDEX

SERVE CREATIVE, EASY, NUTRITIOUS MEALS WITH NITTY GRITTY® COOKBOOKS

Recipes for the Pressure Cooker
The New Blender Book
The Well Dressed Potato
Convection Oven Cookery
The Steamer Cookbook
The Pasta Machine Cookbook
The Versatile Rice Cooker
The Dehydrator Cookbook
Waffles
The Coffee Book
The Bread Machine Cookbook
The Bread Machine Cookbook II
The Bread Machine Cookbook III
The Bread Machine Cookbook IV
The Sandwich Maker Cookbook
The Juicer Book
The Juicer Book II

Bread Baking (traditional), revised
The Kid's Cookbook
No Salt, No Sugar, No Fat Cookbook, revised
Cooking for 1 or 2, revised
Quick and Easy Pasta Recipes, revised
15-Minute Meals for 1 or 2
The 9x13 Pan Cookbook
Extra-Special Crockery Pot Recipes
Chocolate Cherry Tortes and Other Lowfat Delights
Low Fat American Favorites
Low Fat International Cuisine
Now That's Italian!

Fabulous Fiber Cookery
Low Salt, Low Sugar, Low Fat Desserts
Healthy Cooking on the Run, revised
Healthy Snacks for Kids
Muffins, Nut Breads and More
The Barbecue Book
The Wok
Quiche & Soufflé
New Ways to Enjoy Chicken
Favorite Seafood Recipes
New International Fondue Cookbook
Favorite Cookie Recipes
Authentic Mexican Cooking
Fisherman's Wharf Cookbook

Write or call for our free catalog.
BRISTOL PUBLISHING ENTERPRISES, INC.
P.O. Box 1737, San Leandro, CA 94577
(800) 346-4889; in California (510) 895-4461